CW00747491

Stanbrook Abbey

By John Richard Hodges

'My sincere thanks to Sister Margaret Truran OSB, and Sister Philippa Edwards OSB, who lived at Stanbrook for many years and know the Abbey from the inside, so to speak. They have scrutinized the text, and made many comments and suggestions. Any mistakes that remain are the responsibility of the author.'

Contents

Face Page	i
Contents	ii
Dedication	iii
List of colour plates	iv
Plans	v
Bibliography	vii

* *

Introduction: Stanbrook Abbey - Callow End - Worcestershire

Chapter One: The Early History

Chapter Two: Stanbrook Abbey – The Buildings

Chapter Three: Stanbrook Abbey Printing Press

Chapter Four: The Gardens and Park

Chapter Five: Stanbrook Abbey in Yorkshire

For Nick - *A Remarkable Young Man-1979-1998*

There are many people

who come and go in our lives,

a few touch us in ways

that change us forever.

You have made a difference

in my life and I am grateful.

John Richard Hodges ~ 2019

List of Colour Plates

1. Stanbrook Abbey Hotel
2. Views from the Church Tower & Aerial views of the Abbey
3. The Great Hall and former Chapel
4. Clayton and Bell – Stained glass window from the East End of the Great Hall
5. George's Bar & the Minton Tiles in the Cloister
6. St Benedict's Cloister with the mural of St Benedict and the Minton tiles.
7. The Stained Glass in the 'Via Crucis'
8. Entrance door to the Great Hall
9. Pugin Staircase at Stanbrook Abbey
10. St Anne's Hall, the former Chapel & the Thompson Dining Room
11. Bedrooms in the present hotel
12. Former Parlour for visitors to the Abbey, the Mural in the Cellar & the collection of wine bottles
13. 'Hardman & Co.' of Birmingham'- West window
14. 'Boulton' sculpture from the Great Hall
15. Further 'Boulton' carvings from the Great Hall
16. Carvings from the Choir Stalls in the Great Hall
17. Crucifix from the 'Garden of Remembrance'
18. 'Via Crucis' Cloister on an autumn morning
19. Crucifix in the 'Via Crucis' Cloister
20. ' The Best of Friends' poster
21. 'Hardman' Stained glass from the Great Hall showing St John and the Crucifixion
22. The Tombs of Dom Laurence Shepherd & Abbess Gertrude D' Aurillac Dubois
23. Minton floor tiles
24. Cloisters in the Abbey
25. 'Stanbrook Abbey' in Yorkshire
26. The Refectory
27. Caravaggio – 'The Crowning with Thorns' & 'Christ carrying the Cross' by El Greco.
28. The Great Hall & Stanbrook in the snow
29. Stanbrook Abbey Hotel at night & Hardman and Co. window

30. Wedding Marque and Brides Manor
31. The Games Rooms at the hotel
32. The Library Lounge and Brides Manor

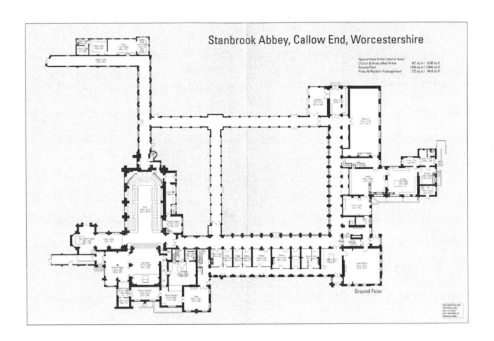

Ground & First Floor Plan including the cellars of the Abbey

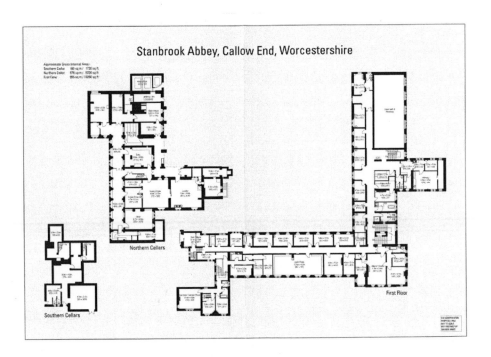

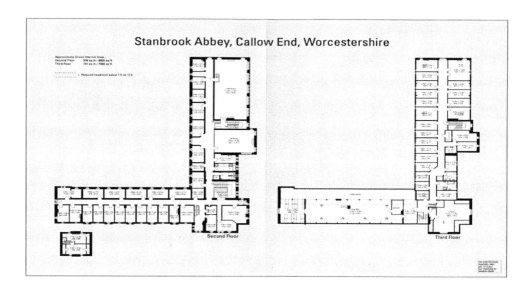

The Second and Third Floor Plan

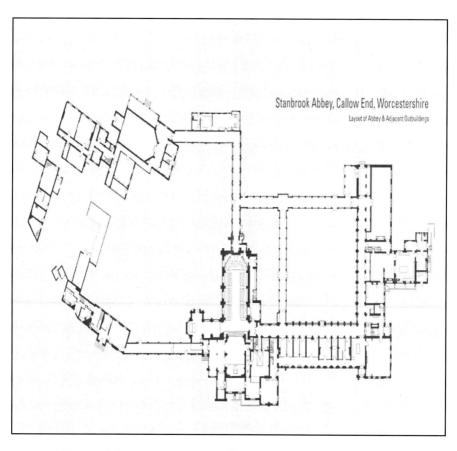

Layout of the ground plan of the Abbey and adjacent outbuildings

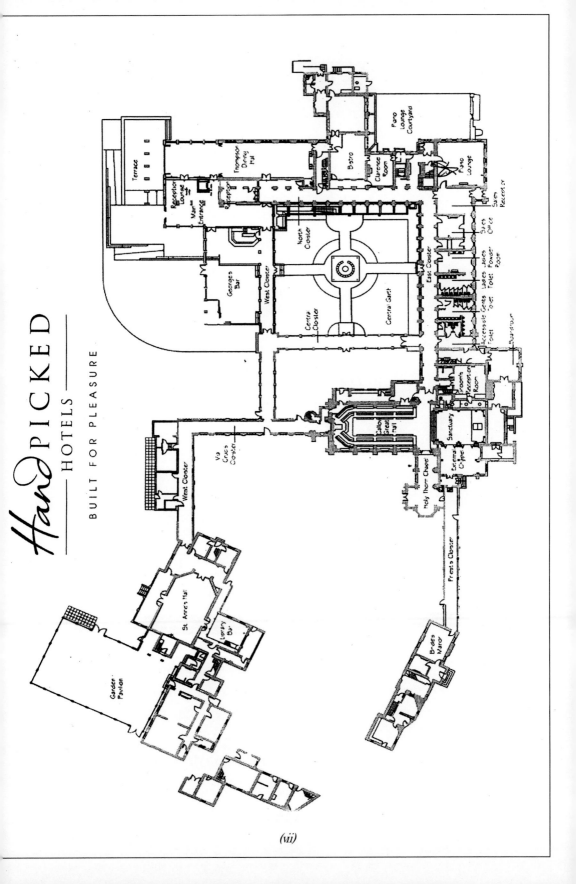

Bibliography – *the following is a select bibliography of the main published sources relating to Stanbrook Abbey and its architectural background.*

Architectural History:

Nikolaus Pevsner, *The Buildings of England: Worcestershire 1968.*

Phoebe Stanton, *Pugin,* 1971.

Anthony Thompson and Joanna Jamieson, *Church Art and Architecture: Reordering of Stanbrook Abbey Church in The Clergy Review,* March 1972, 241-48.

Alexander Wedgwood, *A. W. N. Pugin and the Pugin family, 1985.*

Roderick O'Donnell, *The Later Pugins* in Paul Atterbury and Clive Wainwright (eds.) *Pugin: A Gothic Passion, 1994.*

Howard Colvin, *A Biographical Dictionary of British Architects, 1600-1840 edn 1995.*

Roderick O'Donnell, *The Pugins and the Catholic Midlands, 2002.*

History of the Community:

D. Laurentia McLachlan, *Stanbrook Abbey: a sketch of its History, 1625-1925, 1925.*

Benedictines of Stanbrook (Anon.), *In a Great Tradition: Tribute to Dame Laurentia McLachlan, Abbess of Stanbrook, 1956.*

D. Eanswythe Edwards, *Home at Last: How the Community came to Stanbrook, 1989.*

Listed Buildings and Law:

Charles Mynors, *Listed Buildings, Conservation Area and Monuments,* 3rd edn, 1999.

Stanbrook Abbey, Callow End – Conservation Plan by Michael Hill 2005.

Introduction: Stanbrook Abbey-Callow End – Worcestershire

Stanbrook Abbey in Worcestershire is an abbey originally built as a contemplative house for Benedictine nuns.

An aerial view of Stanbrook Abbey when it was still a Benedictine contemplative house

The original monastic order that came to Stanbrook, was founded in 1625 in Cambrai, Flanders, which was at this time part of the Spanish Netherlands, under the auspices of the *English Benedictine Congregation*. *The English Benedictine Congregation* has now relocated to Wass in the North York Moors National Park.

According to 'Historic England' the buildings at Stanbrook were dated as follows: -

'Stanbrook Hall (the Presbytery and today under 'Handpicked Hotels' the ('Bride's Manor)' C18/early 19 century; Abbey buildings of 1838 by Charles Day; New Church and cloisters of 1869-71 by E. W. Pugin; Holy Thorn Chapel of 1885-86 by P. P. Pugin; Abbey buildings by Peter Paul and Cuthbert Welby Pugin and George Coppinger Ashlin of 1878-80, 1895-98 and 1898-1900: Materials used: Whitewashed brick with slate roofs, red brick with ashlar dressings and tiled roof. Plan (see version at the start of the book):

Single storey, two and three storey ranges with attics and basements set around two open, cloistered quadrangles with the Church and the Via Crucis cloister dividing them.'

(George Coppinger Ashlin – 1837-1921 – was an Irish architect particularly noted for his work on churches and cathedrals. He had an early association with E. W. Pugin.)

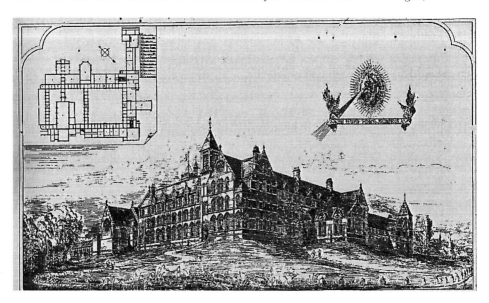

A view of the intended complete monastery as published in 'The Architect' in December 1881. This reproduces the Hemptinne plan in the top left hand corner. Most of what is shown here was eventually built with the exception of the school wing on the right and the top of the bell tower over the main entrance porch. Also, this drawing shows the refectory in a wing projecting at right angles from the north wing, in the location where the kitchens were built: - courtesy of the Stanbrook Abbey Archives and Sister Philippa Edwards & Sister Margaret Truran©

Much of my research has centred on the Conservation plan produced by Michael Hill, a Dip Arch RIBA IHBC, which was produced on behalf of 'The Benedictine Community at Stanbrook Abbey in 2005.' His descriptions of the various parts of the Abbey before the Nuns moved to Yorkshire is of profound importance. Michael Hill's summary of the plan reads as follows:

'Stanbrook Abbey is of national significance as part of the architectural history of the Roman Catholic Revival, and the development of institutional buildings in the 19th century. The abbey church was designed by E. W. Pugin in the late 1860s. He followed the precepts of his influential father A. W. N. Pugin, and the monastic buildings of 1877-80 and the 1890s broadly follow E. W. Pugin's initial proposals, although these were designed and executed by P. P. and C. W. Pugin.' – (Thanks to Michael Hill for permission to use his Plan).

Edward Welby Pugin the English architect and eldest son of Augustus Welby Northmore Pugin and Louise Barton

Whilst Stanbrook Hall is of local significance, its adaption and extension to form the new monastery in the 1830s by Charles Day is of national interest, especially in terms of the architectural style that was adopted. The chapel is of that date and particularly significant in its neoclassical architectural style and the role of Baroque design influences on its interior.

The Abbey Church of Our Lady of Compassion, Stanbrook Abbey, showing the a) original High Altar and reredos, b) the original interior & c) again a different style, later removed.

The present chapel known as 'The Great Hall' in all its magnificence at Stanbrook Abbey

In England, E. W. Pugin's most important convent chapels (both for enclosed Benedictine nuns) are those to be found at *Oulton* in Staffordshire which date from the very start of his career - and in connection with which his father had already been approached – and at *Stanbrook Abbey* in Worcestershire, which extends into his final phase. Internally, 'Oulton' has managed to avoid the damage caused by liturgical re-ordering.

Oulton in Staffordshire

Stanbrook Abbey in Worcestershire

The unspoilt Church of St Mary's, Oulton with the original altar and wall paintings and overleaf the changed church at Stanbrook Abbey

Sadly, the same could not be said about the interior of Stanbrook where the original High Altar and reredos no longer survive, having first suffered mutilation in the late 1930s (long before the Second Vatican Council), and then completely removed – together with the beautiful J. Hardman Powell metal screen in 1971. Then the Minton floor tiles in the chancel – designed by E. W. Pugin & J. H. Powell were replaced with cheap sanitary tiles.

Examples of the 'Minton' tiles at Stanbrook Abbey: - JRH

The John Hardman screen at Stanbrook Abbey removed from the Church in 1971

In other respects, the furnishings at Stanbrook Abbey Church are remarkably well preserved, the Minton floor tiles in the nuns' choir, the Kauri pine choir stalls and the organ case meriting particular mention.

The Kauri pine choir stalls in the Church: - JRH©

The outside had also suffered, even before it was begun. E. W. Pugin's original church was replaced by a somewhat inferior one and even this was altered at the last minute at the behest of the chaplain Dom Laurence Shepherd OSB, who *'at the last moment'* insisted on a clock tower with a dominating stair turret (of which E. W. Pugin strongly disapproved) in place of the intended west end bellcote. The stair turret is actually fairly close in design to the original tower of the Granville Hotel in Ramsgate.

The original Pugin design and the later present day design of the exterior of the church

The original tower at the Granville Hotel in Ramsgate

E. W. Pugin was in fact influenced by the design of a church he saw in Normandy and by the church towers in Belgium, where in 1868 he was building a church. His new design for a tower that would incorporate nine bells '*was a feature in which the architect Edward Welby Pugin took no little pride,*' the Stanbrook Annalist recorded.

Stanbrook is of Particular Ecclesiastical Interest

✦ For having the first monastery of Benedictine nuns in South America. Santa Maria in Sao Paulo, and also fifteen houses in Brazil, Argentina, Uruguay and Chile, have all sprung from this foundation.

The Monastery of St Benedict, Sao Paulo, Brazil

There are regular visitors from South America in search of their roots, wanting to see the place where the Benedictine foundresses were trained between 1907 and 1911, the west window in the church commemorating the foundation, and the grave of one of the foundresses in the cemetery.

- The first monastery of Benedictine nuns in Australia was founded by two English nuns, one originating from Stanbrook. Australian nuns often visit Stanbrook in the summer for this reason.
- The church is of interest because Stanbrook was at the forefront of the 19th century movement to restore Gregorian Chant in monasteries. It was introduced into Catholic parishes during the first half of the 20th century. In the wake of Vatican Council II they incorporated the composition of texts and musical settings into a plainsong liturgy in the vernacular.

* *

Chapter One – The Early History

Stanbrook Abbey was formerly home to an enclosed community of Benedictine nuns belonging to the English Benedictine Congregation. The nine foundresses left England for France in 1623, to be trained under the guidance of English monks. Funds for the foundation were provided by Mr Cresacre More. His daughter Helen was one of the nine foundresses. The More family crest can be seen in the Thompson Dining Hall at the present hotel. It is interesting to note that the party of eight, including Helen More, travelled together and a ninth Englishwomen, Catherine Gascoigne, joined them on route.

The Crest of Cresacre More in the Thompson Dining Hall: - JRH©

The Nuns returned to England after suffering greatly at the time of the French Revolution and being imprisoned for eighteen months. Then they were helped by *Edward Constable* in 1795. They eventually on their return acquired *Stanbrook Hall* set in 22 acres of land. The Georgian manor house had been built in about 1755; the exact date is unknown.

Stanbrook Hall: - JRH

The original 'Refectory' or dining room at Stanbrook Abbey: - courtesy of Neil Styles© This shows the refectory in the later Pugin wing built in 1898, with its 1930s furnishings

Stanbrook Convent: - courtesy of Sister Philippa – Stanbrook 'Wass'©

As there was still a great deal of anti-Catholic feeling in England at this time, to purchase Stanbrook Hall and its grounds needed some undercover dealings and so Dom Bernard Short posed in subterfuge as a country gentleman, while Fathers Birdsall, Barber, Heptonstall and Scott were the monks who later signed the title deeds as joint tenants. It was only after the deeds had been signed that the owner realised that the estate was being purchased to become a convent.

Before moving to Stanbrook, the community had a temporary home at a small country house called *Salford Hall,* Abbots' Salford, Warwickshire, while they looked for somewhere to live in the longer term. From 1606 until the end of the nineteenth century it was owned by the *Stanford family* who were notable Catholics. In the eighteenth century a room in the house was converted to a chapel and served by Benedictine monks. *Robert Berkeley* inherited the property from the Stanfords, arranging for the nuns to move into the building after they had been staying at their first English refuge at Woolton, today part of the City of Liverpool.

* *

An interesting article appeared in the 'Berrow's Worcester Journal' on the 19th June 1869 relating to the new chapel and the bells to be installed in the new tower. The three bells were blessed in June 1869 but soon became nine, a gift from Fr Laurence. He wanted the bells to ring a full octave, as at the Abbey of Solesmes.

INTERESTING CEREMONY AT STANBROOK CONVENT

' It has been found necessary to build a new chapel in the grounds of the Benedictine Convent at Stanbrook, Powick, plans were prepared by Mr Welby Pugin the eminent

architect, and on Tuesday the key stone of the new building was laid. On the previous evening the ceremony of the blessing of the bells for the new chapel was performed according to the rites of the Roman Church by the R.C. Bishop – the Right Rev. Dr Ullathorne.

The newly constructed Church tower and the new bells installed: - JRH©

There are three bells, dedicated respectively to the Blessed Virgin, St. Benedict and St. Scholastica. The three bells were hung from a beam on the lawn in front of the convent and on each side stood the nuns and several children dressed in white, and wearing white veils. Extending in a semi-circle from these were the clergy; the Bishop being enthroned in the centre of the clergy. The bells were wreathed with evergreens, and after they were blessed they rung out a merry peel. Tuesday's ceremony was witnessed by a large number of visitors. The Bishop was enthroned under a canopy, and the service was chanted by the nuns. The order of the ceremony was according to the Roman Pontifical, which directs that on the day before the consecration a wooden cross is to be fixed in the place where the altar is to be; and on the next day the foundation stone must be blessed in the following manner – The Bishop, vested over his rochet, or, if he be religious, over his surplice, with amice, alb, girdle, stole, white cope, and plain mitre, and holding the crosier in his left hand standing, with his mitre, at the place where the church is to be founded, blesses the salt and water, and begins the service by saying 'adjutorium nostrum in nomine Domini.' The celebrant was Dr Ullathorne. The ceremony was very elaborate and impressive. At the close of the ceremony, the visitors were hospitably entertained at the convent by the Lady Abbess. A large number of monks of the Benedictine Order were present. The ceremony was performed within what is called 'the enclosure' and was consequently of a private character.' (Thanks to Sue Campbell for finding me this article)

An article appeared in the *Bells Weekly Messenger* on the 9th September 1871 which concerned the building of the new Benedictine Abbey Church at Callow End in Worcestershire.

'*On Wednesday Dr Ullathorne, assisted by Bishop Browne, of Belmont, consecrated the new church of the Abbey, Stanbrook, near Worcester. The church is but a first instalment of the new Abbey buildings, which when finished, are to accommodate 100 religious, with apartments for the same number of young ladies, who will receive their education in this establishment, under the direction of the nuns. The interior of the new church contains every feature of a monastic church of the Middle Ages. The building will cost about £10,000 and is executed from the designs of Mr E. Welby Pugin.*' (Thanks to Sue Campbell for this article)

The altered 'Pugin' Church at Stanbrook Abbey with the additional spire at the summit: -JRH©

The 'Berrow's Worcester Journal' for the 21st September 1878 mentions the new buildings at Stanbrook, Worcester:

'*New buildings are in the course of erection at St. Mary's Abbey, Stanbrook; they are designed by Messrs. Pugin and Ashley, the builders being Messrs. Wood of Worcester. Anyone who, whilst visiting the ruins of the old abbeys scattered over our land, has observed how close a resemblance of plans exists among them all, and at the same time, how totally different their arrangement is from the ordinary dwelling houses whether ancient or modern, can easily understand how ill-suited to the requirements of monastic* observance must be Stanbrook Hall, a mere ordinary manor house in every point of view, and entirely too small for the number of its inmates; for though presenting to the eye a large pile of buildings, it is in reality very narrow and deficient. The nuns, having been compelled to put up with this abnormal state of things during the years which have elapsed since their first coming into this neighbourhood are now enabled to commence the long desired abbey, designated strictly according to monastic traditions. One wing only of the projected abbey is now in the course of erection. The nuns are anxious not to dismiss the workmen till the whole can be finished; still the want of pecuniary means necessarily deters them from opening the foundations of the rest of the abbey, the entire plans, however, of which are already completed. It may, perhaps be interesting to the neighbourhood to be furnished with a few details as to the previous history of the nuns established here since 1838. The nuns at Stanbrook are Benedictines, a religious order founded in the sixth century at Subiaco, in Italy, and which rapidly spread over the whole of Europe, carrying light and civilisation wherever it appeared. They are the representatives of those who formerly peopled so many abbeys in our land. Driven out of England at the period of religious troubles of the sixteenth century, they took fresh root at Cambray in 1625, when seven English ladies founded an abbey there, embracing the same manner of life as that now followed by the nuns at Stanbrook. Their names were – Miss Helen More, daughter of Mr Cresacre More great-grandson in a direct line of the High Chancellor of England, Sir Thomas More, beheaded in the reign of Henry VIII; Miss Margaret Vavasour, daughter of Mr William Vavasour, of Hazelwood in Yorkshire; Miss Ann Morgan, sister of Mr Thomas Morgan, of Weston, in Warwickshire; Miss Catherine Gascoigne, daughter of Sir John Gascoigne of Barnbow, in Yorkshire. Miss Grace and Miss Ann More, cousins to Miss Helen More, above named; Miss Frances Watson, daughter of Mr Richard Watson, a Bedfordshire squire. With these ladies were associated Mary Hoskins and Jane Martin for the service of the community in quality of 'lay-sisters.' Then, as now, these religious devoted themselves to the great work of prayer, at the same time educating a limited number of young ladies in all Christian and polite literature, fitting them to become, in after life, edifying and useful members of society. At the period of the French Revolution after suffering imprisonment at Compiegne, whence they were released by the death of Robespierre, sentenced though they had been to the guillotine, the 'English Dames', as they were called, once more set foot on their native soil, and were for a time most hospitably received and powerfully protected by the Duchess of Buckingham. Whilst temporarily resident at Woolton in Lancashire, they were invited in 1807, by Mr Robert Berkeley of Spetchley, to accept of a manor (at the time in his possession) near Evesham known as 'Salford House' which he generously allowed them to have rent-free for the term of his life.

Spetchley Park in Worcestershire is one of the Berkeley family homes, situated close to Stanbrook

But before his death, their number having increased, and their fortunes bettered, they purchased 'Stanbrook Hall', whither they removed in 1838, at which time they were twenty-three in community. Stanbrook Hall at the time the nuns bought it belonged to Mr Abraham Thompson, its former possessors for many years having been the family of Harris – Communicated.'

Stanbrook Hall today, the former manor house known today as 'Bride's Manor'

The Hall was known as the Novitiate in the time of the Abbey – a place to house novice nuns: - courtesy of Sister Philippa – Stanbrook© -This small school block known as 'The Old House' was built in 1838 as an extension to Stanbrook Hall. The architect was Charles Day. The school closed in 1918 and from 1935-86 the upper part of the building served as the noviciate

An interesting article appeared in the 'South Wales Daily News' on the 13ᵗʰ December 1897 regarding a new Abbess at Stanbrook who had come originally from Cardiff in South Wales. The article makes for some interesting reading:

A CARDIFF LADY ENTHRONED

'*St Peter's Chair, the monthly organ of Roman Catholicism in Cardiff, publishes in its Christmas number a highly interesting account of the benediction and enthronement of the new Lady Abbess of St Mary's Abbey, Stanbrook, Worcestershire, last month. The matter derives special interest locally from the fact that the lady elected by her community is, says 'St Peter's Chair' the Right Rev. Dame Cecilia Heywood, resident in Cardiff before her entrance into religion, and well known as the sister of Henry Heywood Esq., J.P., Witla Court, St. Mellon's. The description of the solemn function, presumably written by Rev. Father Cormack, who was present as chaplain to the Heywood family, states that the Bishop of Birmingham pontificated on the occasion. It goes on to say: -'Tierce having been sung at 10 o'clock, the Bishop then vested and proceeded to sing Mass. As the appointed time, viz., just before the Gospel, the Abbess-elect came from the choir, left the enclosure and was conducted by two ladies, Mrs H. Heywood and Miss Heywood of Witla Court, to the Bishop seated on his faldstool* (a folding chair used by a bishop when not occupying the throne or when officiating in a church other than his own) -. *on the predella of the altar steps,* (a step or platform on which an altar is placed.)

An example of a typical 'faldstool'

There with the black veil falling over her face, the Abbess-elect knelt down and from an engrossed parchment, sealed with a seal pendant, read the usual oath of fealty taken by an exempt Abbess to the Holy Father and to the Ordinary. Then placing both hands on the Gospel she completed the oath and handed the parchment to the Bishop. After this followed the chanting of the Litanies by the choir of nuns and the clergy alternatively, the Abbess-elect prostrated herself in the Sanctuary (The most holy part of the Church) meanwhile. This solemn supplication was a most impressive feature of the rite. At the prescribed portion of the Litanies (a series of petitions for use in church services or processions, usually recited by the clergy and responded to in a recurring formula by the people), the Abbess, still prostrate, was blessed by the Bishop. Then the Abbess having arisen there followed the imposition of the Bishop's hands on her head with appropriate prayers imploring the Divine guidance and council for her in the discharge of her office. The tradition of the 'Book of Rules' fitly closed this part of the ceremonial, after which the Abbess, accompanied by her ladies-in-waiting, retired to the Epistle side of the Sanctuary to a kneeling-desk prepared for her.

Some examples of a 'prayer-desk' or 'prie-dieu'

The splendid carving of the phoenix and her chicks from a 'prie-dieu' found at Stanbrook: -JRH

The Prayer-Stool at Stanbrook, with the charming carvings of the phoenix and her chicks. The phoenix is a ninth-century poem in Old English depicting the life, death and resurrection of the mythical phoenix bird, complete with a religious commentary at the end....The symbolism openly conveys the resurrection of Christ leading to the salvation of mankind, depicting their entrance into Heaven: -JRH

* *

At the offertory the newly-blessed Abbess returned to the altar steps being preceded by two esquires, Messrs Henry and Alfred Heywood, who bore lighted torches, which the Abbess presented separately to the Bishop, the Abbess having received Holy Communion the Mass was concluded. The Bishop then enthroned the Abbess in the Sanctuary and placed in her hands the pastoral staff of the Abbey, immediately intoning the 'Te Deum,' during the singing of which the Lady Abbess was conducted back to the enclosure of the Monastery in the same way as she had left it.'

An example of an abbess's crozier or pastoral staff – her jurisdiction is different from that of the bishop. This illustration shows Eufemia Szaniawska, Abbess of the Benedictine Monastery in Nieswiez with a crosier, c1768: National Museum in Warsaw©

Some examples of different pastoral staffs held by the Bishop in Church services

The Abbess having taken her place in the choir all the sisters advanced to receive from her the kiss of peace, which was the most touching sight, especially when two of the oldest nuns, leaning on the arms of younger sisters, one of them also supporting her tottering steps with a long staff, slowly approached the Abbess's stall at the west end of the long choir and then returned to their own seats. Besides the friends of the Abbess who took actual part in the function, there were present Miss Gilda Heywood, Mr and Mrs Charles Heywood and Mr Willie Heywood of Swansea.'

* *

Chapter Two: Stanbrook Abbey – The Buildings

Postcard of Stanbrook Abbey dated 14ᵗʰ August 1955 (aerial Pictorial Ltd, 137 Regent Street, London): - courtesy of Andrew Bridges, Hereford©

Aerial View of Stanbrook at the time of the sale of the Abbey showing its spectacular position in the Worcestershire Countryside (see colour plate): - courtesy of Neil Styles©

The Callow Great Hall:

This was the former chapel of the abbey and was consecrated in 1871. With its high vaulted ceiling, it is a wonderful example of the Pugin style.

Callow Great Hall, the main Church at Stanbrook Abbey as it appears today: - courtesy of Handpicked Hotels©

It was Edward Welby Pugin - 1834-1875 who was largely responsible for drawing up the plans for the Benedictine Abbey at Stanbrook:

Edward Welby Pugin – was an English architect and the eldest son of *Augustus Welby Northmore Pugin* and *Louisa Barton*. His father was the famous architect and designer of 'Neo-Gothic architecture' and after his death in 1852, Edward took up his father's successful practice. Edward, like his father died fairly young in 1875 aged just 41 years of age. He had by this time designed and completed more than one hundred Catholic churches.

Edward Welby's work was mostly in his native British Isles, but he had commissions for his unique style from countries throughout Western Europe, Scandinavia and as far away as North America.

Edward Welby Pugin - 1834 - 1875

Some of the impressive places where Edward Welby worked in England can be shown in the following list:

- *St Begh's Church, Whitehaven, Cumberland (1868)*
- *St Mary of Furness Roman Catholic Church, Barrow-in-Furness, Lancashire (1866-67)*

- *St Mary's Church, Cleator, Cumberland (1872)*
- *Our Lady and St Michael's Church, Workington, Cumberland (1876)*
- *St Patrick's Wolverhampton (demolished)*
- *1853: Our Lady Immaculate and St Cuthbert, Crook, Co. Durham*
- *1856: Shrewsbury Cathedral, the Cathedral Church of Our Lady Help of Christians and Saint Peter of Alcantara, Town Walls, Shrewsbury (built as a cathedral)*

The Catholic Cathedral in Shrewsbury

- *1856: Our Lady Immaculate, St Domingo Road, Everton, Liverpool. Demolished. Lady Chapel of scheme for Liverpool Cathedral*
- *1856: St Vincent de Paul, St James Street, Liverpool*
- *1857: Holy Cross, Croston, Lancashire. Small estate church*
- *1857–59: Our Lady and St Hubert, Great Harwood, Lancashire*
- *1859: Belmont Abbey, Hereford, Herefordshire (the Abbey Church was built as the pro-Cathedral for Wales)*

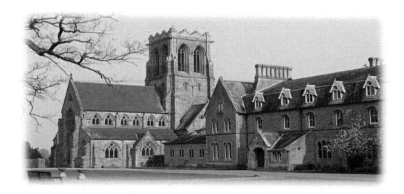

Belmont Abbey, Hereford

- *1860: Octagonal Chapter House, Mount Saint Bernard Abbey, Leicestershire*
- *1859-60: Our Lady of la Salette, Liverpool*
- *1860: St Mary Immaculate, Warwick*

St Mary Immaculate - Warwick

- *1860-61: St Anne, Westby, Kirkham, Lancashire*
- *1861: St Edward, Thurloe Street, Rusholme, Manchester*
- *1861-65: St Michael, West Derby Road, Everton, Liverpool*
- *1862: St Anne, Chester Road, Stretford, near Manchester*
- *1862: St Austin, Wolverhampton Road, Stafford*
- *1863: St Peter, Greengate, Salford, Lancashire*
- *1863: SS Henry and Elizabeth, Sheerness, Kent*
- *1863: Convent of Our Lady of Charity and Refuge, Bartestree, Herefordshire (Subsequently, converted to flats)*
- *1863: St Joseph, Bolton Road, Anderton, Chorley, Lancashire*
- *1863-64: Monument to Everard Aloysius Lisle Phillipps, VC, Cademan Wood, Whitwick, Leicestershire*
- *1864: Our Lady and All Saints, New Road, Stourbridge, Worcestershire*

Our Lady and All Saints - Stourbridge

- *1864: St Marie, Lugsdale Road, Widnes, Cheshire (redundant)*
- *1864: Our Lady of Redemption, Wellesley Road, Croydon*
- *1864: St Hubert, Dunsop Bridge, Yorkshire*
- *1864-66: Augustinian Priory, school and church (St Monica), Hoxton Square, London*
- *1865: St Mary, Euxton, Lancashire*
- *1865: St Catherine, Kingsdown, Kent*
- *1865–66: Mayfield Boys' Orphanage (later Mayfield College, from 2007 converted to residential apartments as Mayfield Grange), Mayfield, Sussex*
- *1865–67: St Joseph, York Road, Birkdale, Southport, Lancashire*
- *1866: Euxton Hall Chapel, Euxton, near Chorley, Lancashire*
- *1866: St Francis Monastery, Gorton, Manchester*

St Francis Monastery, Gorton, Manchester

- *1866: Our Blessed Lady and St Joseph, Leadgate, Durham*
- *1866: Chancel and transepts to Mount St Mary's Church, Leeds*
- *1866–68: Meanwood Towers, Meanwood, Leeds*
- *1866–67: St Mary, Duke Street, Barrow-in-Furness, Lancashire*
- *1866–67: St Michael and All Angels, Mortuary Chapel and Knill Memorial, Brockley Cemetery, London, destroyed by bombing in 1944*
- *1866–67: Church of St Thomas of Canterbury and the English Martyrs, Preston, Lancashire, (extended in 1887–88)*

The Church of St Thomas of Canterbury and the English Martyrs, Preston

- *1867: St Paul's, Maison Dieu Road, Dover, Kent*
- *1867–68: St Mary, Fleetwood, Lancashire*
- *1867–68: All Saints', Barton-upon-Irwell, Eccles, Greater Manchester*
- *1867–68: All Saints' Church in Urmston, Greater Manchester*
- *1867–71: Our Lady and St Paulinus, Dewsbury, West Yorkshire*
- *1868: Two colleges at Mark Cross, Sussex*
- *1868: St Begh, Coach Road, Whitehaven, Cumberland*
- *1869–72: Our Lady of the Sacred Heart, Cleator, Cumberland*
- *1869: Granville Hotel, Ramsgate, Kent*
- *1871: Stanbrook Abbey, Powick, Worcestershire*
- *1873: St Mary's Church, Brierley Hill*
- *1875 Edward Welby Pugin dies*
- *1875: St Anne Rommer, Highfield Road, Rockferry, Birkenhead, Wirral, Cheshire designed by E.W. Pugin*
- *1875–76: The English Martyrs, London. E.W. Pugin design*
- *1876: Our Lady Star of the Sea, Workington. E.W. Pugin design*

- *1877: St Mary's Church, Warrington, Cheshire. E.W. Pugin design*

The Church at Stanbrook, (known today at 'The Callow Great Hall'), is comprised of three chapels. The main body of the Church known as the 'Choir', is where the nuns would sit to hear the services. They entered originally via the west entrance, behind where the abbatial throne now is situated.

The Abbatial Throne in the Church at Stanbrook: - JRH©

The present entrance into the 'Callow Great Hall' with the ornate stoups on either side. These once contained holy water that the nuns used to make the sign of the cross before entering the church: - courtesy of Neil Styles- Photographer©

Up the steps, in the east end of the church, was the 'Extern Chapel' where the priests gave services screened off from the nuns. The priest entered from the presbytery via the priest's cloister or from the sacristy. The original wrought iron sanctuary screen was designed by *Pugin* and made by *J. H. Powell of Birmingham,* and the insertion of new screens of a modern design separated the sanctuary from the extern chapel.

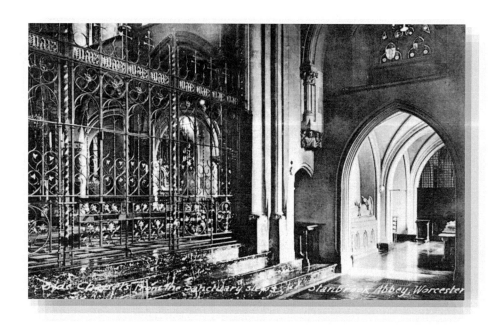

The side chapel off the choir - the Holy Thorn Chapel - with the fine 'Hardman' iron screen and the 'Sanctuary' from the Sacred Heart Chapel with the old altar now removed: - courtesy of Ray Jones©
The original altar and decorative scheme of 1877-78 by Clayton and Bell were lime washed by the
1950s

The High Altar at Stanbrook Abbey: - courtesy of 'Handpicked Hotels' & PFA©

c1871 view of the church interior showing the original sanctuary layout, complete with the elaborate altar and reredos, and the screen by Hardman Powell of Birmingham. The sanctuary was reordered in the 1930s, and again in 1971. The photograph was taken by T. Bennett of Worcester to commemorate the opening of the church: - courtesy of Michael Hill & Stanbrook Abbey Archives©

The site of the original High Altar at Stanbrook Abbey. The various altars have been removed and sadly some of the original wall paintings and even some of the Minton tiles were replaced in the 70s with plain clay tiles: - JHH©

Close to the main altar is the small area which contains the 'confessional' which was installed in 1987 to allow face-to-face confession – for use by the faithful, not by the nuns as it lies outside the enclosure. Only a priest can hear confession; no woman, not even an Abbess can do so! - JRH©

The Sacred Heart Chapel (or Extern Chapel) lies to the right of the sanctuary. Its altar has been removed and also the stained glass in the enormous south window. This image shows what it would have looked like:

Early postcard of the Sacred Heart Chapel: - courtesy of Ray Jones© The Chapel today with a 'squint' to watch the service in the main Chapel: - JRH

The small side chapel which we see today is built externally in the style of a medieval reliquary shrine. Here at Stanbrook it is called the *Chapel of the Holy Thorn*. It contains the tombs of *Dom Laurence Shepherd* (d.1885), who drafted the first plan of the expanded Abbey and *Abbess Gertrude D'Aurillac Dubois* (d. 1897). The chapel once held a relic of the *Holy Thorn* from Glastonbury Abbey – said to have come from the crown of thorns Christ wore at his crucifixion.

Sister Margaret has told me an interesting account of what must be called a miracle. This took place on 25th November 1889. Dame Teresa Bradley, unable to walk without severe pain and extremely weak after months of being unable to retain hardly any food, was brought to the tombs in the Chapel of Thorns, where she with help knelt and prayed. She rose from her knees, able to walk easily and firmly, without any sign of the previous physical weakness. The doctor attested to the miraculous nature of her recovery.

Father Laurence, Stanbrook's chaplain (1863-85), is honoured for having erected the church and the first wing of the monastery. He was also responsible for the interior design of the church and the raising of funds to build the church. He himself gave the organ, clock and bells.

Dom Laurence Shepherd - 1825-1885) - *'I did everything in my power to develop the monastic spirit there.'*

'The portrait of Fr Laurence, an Ampleforth monk, has caught his sensitive, gentle, yet playful character; perhaps also his simplicity of heart. He helped to supervise the building of the church at Stanbrook Abbey, climbing it was said fearlessly up the scaffolding and up the tower turret to set a cross at the very summit.'

Father Laurence's cross at the very summit of the steep tower at Stanbrook Church Tower: - JRH

Father Laurence completes the trio of holy men who have played an important role in the community's history to date. Appointed vicar, or chaplain in 1863, he found at Stanbrook a desire to restore the full monastic observance that had been rudely shattered when the nuns had been expelled from Cambrai in 1793.

With great patience and kindness he passed on the enthusiasm that he had received first - hand from Dom Prosper Gueranger, abbot of Solesmes; an understanding that the public choral celebration of Mass and the Office is not only of prime importance to the monastic day as an act of divine worship, but also central to the individual's spiritual growth. He provided the means to implement this vision with a grounding in Latin and a fine patristic library, together with a church where the liturgy could be celebrated with beauty and solemnity. He also had the support of Abbess Gertrude d'Aurillac Dubois, who was the Abbess from 1872-1897.

The tomb of Dom Laurence Shepherd in the Chapel of the Holy Thorn

Detail on the tomb of Dom Laurence Shepherd: - JRH©

The three carved niches in the tomb of Dom Laurence Shepherd show: Left: Jacob dreaming; above him are two angels descending and ascending the long flight of stairs to the rays of the sun in the top right-hand corner. The scene alludes to Fr Laurence's building of the abbey church. His Christian name was James (= Jacob).

In the centre niche there is *Christ the Good Shepherd*, an allusion to Fr Laurence's surname.

On the right is the *Sower*, wearing the habit of an English Benedictine monk. This is a reference to Fr Laurence's twenty-two years of spiritual teaching at Stanbrook, and to his translation of Dom Gueranger's 'The Liturgical Year.' The volumes are still in print over a hundred and fifty years later.

* *

While the Chapel of the Holy Thorn was being built, the Prioress, Placida Jackson, managed to secure a second vault for Abbess Gertrude, without her knowing!

Abbess Gertrude d'Aurillac Dubois (Abbess 1872-97), Father Laurence's co-worker, was responsible for the second wing of the monastery. The recumbent effigy (Derbyshire alabaster) surmounting her tomb was modelled by Dame Beatrice Brown of Stanbrook, professed the year (1897) that her Abbess died. When the tomb was completed it was on display for two days, the 6th and 7th of March 1901, at Holley Lodge Studio, Fulham Road, London, where it attracted 450 visitors and featured in an article in the *Daily Chronicle* and in *the Worcester Chronicle for 16th March 1901.*

'Women have not often been distinguished, or even conspicuous, in sculpture, so that a special interest is attached to the tomb of the late Lady Abbess d'Aurillac Dubois, of Stanbrook, near Worcester, which was in view last week at Holley Lodge Studio, Fulham Road, London, for it was both designed and executed by women. The figure of the Abbess, who lies outstretched upon her tomb, in much the position of the old Crusaders on theirs,

her head a little lifted on a cushion, her robes lying in long, straight folds, is the work of Dame Beatrice, one of the Benedictine nuns at the abbey. It has a noble dignity in its simplicity, and the face is full of character, serene and peaceful in its strength. The little bas-reliefs that decorate the alabaster base are also modelled by Dame Beatrice, while the base itself was designed and the entire tomb executed by Miss Abbot and Miss Ferguson, with whom she worked before entering the convent.' (Thanks to Sue Campbell for finding this article and Sister Margaret of Stanbrook).

The table tomb of Abbess Gertrude d'Aurillac Dubois; the charming crozier with its crook resting on her pillow: - JRH©

Abbess Gertrude is portrayed wearing her monastic cowl and abbatial insignia that is the pectoral cross, amethyst ring and crozier. They are significant because she was solemnly blessed in 1895 as abbess for life, the first such among Benedictines in this country since the Reformation.

Historic England wrote about the Chapel of the Holy Thorn:

'The Chapel of the Holy Thorn was added to the south side by P. P. Pugin in 1885 and is built externally in the form of a medieval reliquary shrine. It contains two recumbent effigies, that to Dom Laurence Shepherd (d. 1885) by P. P. Pugin, carved by Boulton and that to Abbess Gertrude D'Aurillac Dubois (d.1897) by Dame Beatrice Brown OSB. The altar has paired niches at either side of a central quatrefoil. On the surface is a tabernacle of alabaster with a silver door set with garnets showing a Pelican in her Piety. The reredos takes the form of a Pieta set in a deep foiled niche with a richly carved arch at either end and below which are columns of coloured marble.'

It needs to be noted that the Holy Thorn Chapel was built in honour of the relic of the Holy Thorn, but this was not the relic inserted into the altar. In the seventeenth century, the relic of the Holy Thorn was inserted into a reliquary that has the form of a monstrance for veneration.

Wikipedia gives the following definition of a 'monstrance;

'A monstrance, also known as an ostensorium (or an ostensory), is the vessel used in Roman Catholic, Old Catholic and Anglican churches for the more convenient exhibition of some object of piety, such as the consecrated Eucharist host during Eucharistic adoration or Benediction of the Blessed Sacrament. It is also used as a reliquary for the public display of relics of some saints. The word 'monstrance' comes from the Latin word 'monstrare, while the word 'ostensorium' came from the Latin word 'ostendere'. Both terms meaning 'to show', are used for vessels intended for the exposition of the Blessed Sacrament, but 'ostensorium' has only this meaning.'

Some examples of a 'monstrance' or 'ostensorium'

The Altar in the Chapel of the Holy Thorn which once contained a relic, a thorn which was said to have come from the Crown of Thorns which was placed on Christ's head at the time of the Crucifixion: - JRH

Detail on the altar of the Holy Thorn: - JRH©

This chapel designed by P. P. Pugin in 1885 was erected in honour of the relic of the Holy Thorn that belonged to Glastonbury Abbey before the Reformation. The deep moulded carving around the main arch depicts 7 archangels: Michael at the top as befits the head, wearing chain mail, a sword and shield. On the left from the onlookers point of view is Gabriel holding a lily. There are 2 other depictions of Raphael opposite on the other side, holding a fish, as in the book of Tobit. The archangels' wings, extended over their heads, are delightfully treated. Note the thorn branch interwoven between the foliage and lilies (with tongues) below the archangels

Part of the Reredos in the Chapel of the Holy Thorn. At the centre, recessed within a deep foiled arch, is a Pietà, reflecting the dedication of the altar to Our Lady of Pity. The image of a mother cradling her dead son in her lap, in parallel and contrast with the Virgin and Child of Nativity scenes, became popular in the late middle ages. Above are 7 archangels, who 'stand before the Lord; (Apoc. 8:2). Below are 7 angels interceding for the Benedictine Congregation, especially the Community of Our Lady of Consolation, titular of Stanbrook Abbey

Below the plinth on which the Pietà rests are 7 stone angels, three-quarter size, with different faces. Each bears a shield representing (left to right): St Gerard, Comte d'Aurillac, ancestor of Abbess Gertrude d'Aurillac, the five monasteries of the English Benedictine Congregation, monasteries at the time which included: St Edmund's, Douai; St Gregory's, Downside; Our Lady of Consolation, Stanbrook: St Laurence's, Ampleforth; St Michael's, Belmont, St Thomas More, ancestor of the community's first foundress, Dame Gertrude More.

Details of the altar of the Holy Thorn Chapel: - JRH©

The altar itself in the Chapel is dedicated to Our Lady of Pity.

Thorns are the subject of the altar frontal with:

1. The centre niche, quatrefoil: *Ecce Homo* Christ seated and crowned with thorns and blindfolded.

2. In the left niche can be seen paired arches: *The Sacrifice of Isaac.* Isaac stands besides logs stacked for a burnt offering and a knife. Abraham is shown disentangling a woolly ram caught in a nearby thorn bush.

3. In the right niche: *Adam digging thorns & An Angel with a flaming sword guarding the gates of Paradise.*

The Tabernacle, is of a Hardman, Powell & Co. design and is constructed of alabaster.

Peter Paul Pugin – 1851- March 1904 – was an English architect and the son of Augustus Welby Pugin by his third wife Jane Knill. He was the half-brother of the architect and designer who had been responsible for much of the Abbey at Stanbrook, Edward Welby Pugin.

Peter Paul Pugin, with his wife Agnes Bird and two of their children c1890s

Peter Paul Pugin was only a year old when his father died. When he grew up he became a junior partner in 'Pugin & Pugin', the family architectural firm. The senior partner at this time was his half-brother Edward Welby Pugin.

When Edward Welby died suddenly in the June of 1875, as a result of overwork and the 'injudicious use of chloral hydrate' the main responsibility for the practice passed to Peter Paul Pugin.

Chloral Hydrate: is a germinal diol with the formula $C_2H_3Cl_3O_2$. It is a colourless solid. It has limited use as a sedative and hypnotic pharmaceutical drug. It is also a useful laboratory chemical reagent and precursor. It is derived from chloral (trichloroacetaldehyde) by the addition of one equivalent of water.

Although Peter Paul's offices remained in London and Liverpool, his practice was largely Scottish, and he also maintained an office in Glasgow. Peter Paul's earlier churches were strongly influenced by his father and brother, but by the 1880s he had developed a very recognisable curvilinear style, usually in red sandstone with elaborate altarpieces in coloured marbles.

Caravaggio – The Crowning with Thorns – 1603: -

The organ case in the main church is of Kauri Pine – The Agathis robusta, or the Queensland Kauru pine or smooth-barked kauri is a coniferous tree in the family 'Araucariaceae'. It has a disjunct distribution occurring in Papua New Guinea and Queensland, Australia.

The case is carved with trumpeter angels in roundels together with a passage from Psalm 150, *'Omnis spiritis laudet Dominum' – let every spirit praise the Lord.* The organ has recently undergone restoration and is still used today for services and weddings in the chapel.

The fine Nicholson & Co. organ and the carved stone angels on either side: - JRH©

It was built by Nicholson & Co. in Malvern. A young Edward Elgar learned to play on a Nicholson organ in Worcester, where his father was the organist.

Nicholson & Co. – Malvern

The company was established in Worcester in 1841 by John Nicholson. The name Nicholson & Co. has become synonymous with beautifully toned, comfortable, long-lived, reliable pipe organs which display the highest standards of design, craftsmanship and finish. For over 175 years Nicholson & Co. have created instruments of distinction for Cathedrals, churches, colleges, schools and private clients as well as undertaking the historical restoration and renovation of many hundreds of organs throughout the United Kingdom and overseas.

Nicholson and Co. also built a moveable organ for nearby Worcester Cathedral. Thanks for the research by Dr David Morrison the Cathedral Librarian:

'For music festivals in the second half of the 19th century, yet another specially made organ was built at the west end by Nicholson. Doubtless this third organ was dismantled after each of the music festivals'.

One of the small movable organs constructed by Nicholson and Co. of Malvern

The stained glass in the great west window of the church is the work of Hardman & Co. of Birmingham, 1913. Stained glass for this window had been in mind from the very beginning of the building of the abbey, but funds had not been found at that time.

The window commemorates Stanbrook's foundation in 1911 of the monastery of Santa Maria in Sao Paulo, in Brazil, the first house of Benedictine nuns (as opposed to Benedictine sisters) in the whole of America.

Santa Maria's titular, 'Our Lady of the Immaculate Conception' appears above four scenes evocative of the prioress, Dame Domitilla Tolhurst of Stanbrook, who died at sea on 15th October 1911 within sight of Brazil. Mr Bernard Tolhurst gave the window in memory of his sister.

Details of the 14th century style, are as follows:

1. The large foliated circle at the head of the window shows Mary Immaculate as 'The Woman' of chapter 12 of the Apocalypse, 'at the end of time. 'It had long been considered a suitable design for the West window - in Christian art, the West window traditionally depicts the 'Last Judgement' or 'The Last Times.' It fitted the choice of Santa Maria's titular - the sun (red) surrounds her and the moon below.

2) Other subjects were chosen to suit the life of Dame Domitilla's life:

    a)   Left of the two long trefoiled cusped lights: Purification of Our Lady. Dame Domitilla entering Stanbrook on the 2nd February 1887. Our Lady is shown placing her son in the hands of the priest. A basket with a pair of turtle doves (left); balanced (right) by a basket of blue (for the Virgin Mary) and white flowers (for St Joseph). There is also a shown a menorah.

    b)   Right Light: Epiphany. Dame Domitilla was professed on the 8th January 1889, during the Epiphany Octave. Mary is seated with her Son in her lap; the three kings kneel before her with gifts for the newborn king. A sceptre and crown can be seen at the base- tiny stars shine through Mary to the Christ. Below can be seen two subjects which relate to Dame Domitilla's death:

    c)   Left: there are two subjects. The first shows Peter walking on the water and the death of Dame Domitilla at sea. The figure of Jesus is prominent, taking Peter by the hand. Note the details on the boat's rigging and mast and the pulling on the ropes, and the rudder, not an oar.

d) Right: five wise virgins, with lamps brilliantly alight. The divine Bridegroom is receiving them into heaven through the open gate. There is a border of tiny roses.

The installation of the stained glass was completed in November 1913. In 1988 the glass was removed for restoration by Hardman and replaced on 31ˢᵗ May, the Feast of the Visitation of Our Lady.

Experts on stained glass, state the workmanship is very fine, with the colour, the detail and the superb delineation of the different faces being excellent. It is thought to have been crafted for Hardman by Dunstan Powell, with several other workmen at the company being involved. For example, the noses of the virgins are in the style of J. Hardman Powell (d.1895); the noses of the Magi in the style of Dunstan Powell.

The stunning East Window as with the other stained glass in the church was designed by *'Hardman & Co. of Birmingham'*, who were the long-term collaborators of the Pugin family, most notably on the Houses of Parliament, and other examples such as in Worcester Cathedral where the West Window which has recently been restored is the pride of the Cathedral. Tewkesbury Abbey also has Hardman windows.

The magnificent 'Hardman and Co.' West Window was paid for by Lord Dudley in 1874 in Worcester Cathedral. Largely designed by Sir George Gilbert Scott, it represents scenes from the Book of Genesis, including the 6 days of Creation with the story of Adam and Eve in the centre lights 'Courtesy of the Dean and Chapter of Worcester Cathedral©

The 'Face of Christ' (normally so high up it is difficult to see) during restoration in 2017. It is part of the Hardman & Co. splendid West Window in Worcester Cathedral

* *

Hardman & Co. window in Stanbrook showing Christ and his favourite disciple John at the Last Supper. In the cusped foils, the 'Paraclete' in the form of a dove, overshadows the scene, and two angels look on in adoration: - JRH©

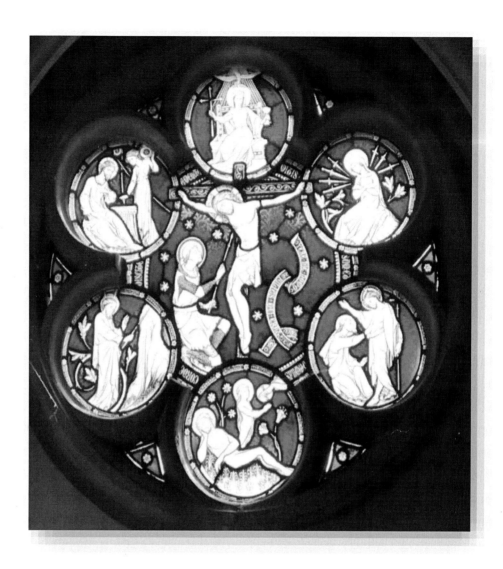

Another Hardman & Co. window at Stanbrook, showing the rose window in the south wall of the Sacred Heart Chapel/Extern Chapel. It presents themes associated with the theology of the Sacred Heart- Longinus with a spear opens Christ's sacred side and heart: - JRH©

The centre light has the subject of the 'Crucifixion'. Longinus with a spear opens Christ's sacred side and heart. His words are sculpted on the scroll, *vere hic homo Filius Dei erat – Truly this man was the Son of God.*

The six foils display the main scenes and symbols associated with the Sacred Heart:

1) Bottom: Adam is asleep; Eve issuing from his side, and with her hands joined, gazes at the hand surrounded by a 'nimbus' that extends from heaven, a mysterious representation of the Creator.

2) Top: Holy Mother Church, represented as a Queen enthroned and crowned with a diadem. In her right hand she holds a cross and in her left a chalice. The Holy Spirit portrayed as a dove, overshadows her.

3) Left, bottom: Moses striking a rock, from which gushes forth water.

4) Left, top: Samaritan woman with Jesus at Jacob's well.

5) Top, right: Our Lady of Sorrows, with seven swords piercing her breast and heart.

6) Right, bottom: Jesus after the Resurrection, instructing Thomas to place his hand in the wound in his side.

* *

The magnificent east window in the sanctuary (or chancel) of the Church: - JRH

Centre Light: Our Lady of Consolation. When the community now at Stanbrook was founded in Cambrai, it was placed under her protection. There are Benedictine nuns kneeling on either side of her. Above their heads are the words *'Consolamini, Consolamini'* *(Isaiah 40)*.

The eight surrounding small foils bear the words 'Ipse est pax vestra qui fecit utraque unum' – *He himself is your peace, who has made you both one.'* (Ephesians 2:14). The Benedictine motto is *Pax/Peace.*

The eight foils depict scenes from the life of the Blessed Virgin Mary:

a) Top: The Assumption. Mary is shown rising from the tomb, and accompanied on either side by an angel

b) Bottom: At the foot of her Son's Cross

c) Top right: The Birth of Jesus, with Joseph with an ox and ass

d) Centre right: Burial of Jesus

e) Bottom right: The taking down of Jesus from the Cross

f) Bottom left: Meeting Jesus on the way to Calvary

g) Centre left: Gabriel appears to Mary at the Annunciation

h) Top left: The Descent of the Holy Spirit at Pentecost

In the outer cusps are roses, which are one of the symbols of the Virgin Mary (for the same reason roses are carved along the desks of the front and the back rows of the choir stalls.)

* *

Evidence of the nuns' dedication to their faith can be seen on the floor of the pews where hours of kneeling in daily worship have created significant grooves over the years.

Grooves can be seen in the honey-toned New Zealand satinwood stalls where the nuns have prayed for many hours since the church has been built: - JRH©

The splendid carved dragon and poppy head bench ends on the choir stalls in the 'Great Hall.': -
JRH©

The balcony overlooking the Choir where the sick and infirm nuns could watch and take part in the services below: - JRH©

The view from the balcony looking down into the main Church: - JRH©

All of the original floor tiles are *Minton*. *Mintons Ltd* was another favoured collaborator of *Augustus Pugin*. Another notable example of Minton tiles can be found in the United States Capital Building in Washington DC.

Examples of the Minton tiles in the Capital Building in Washington DC

The Capital Building in Washington DC, USA

Similar Minton tiles can be seen in St George's Hall in Liverpool which show a magnificent example of this type of art and are very similar in design to the ones from Washington DC.

The splendid Minton Tiles in the Great Hall of St George's Hall in Liverpool

Minton tiles were manufactured by the Minton Hollins tile factory in Stoke on Trent which, by the 1890s, was producing two million tiles a month. Minton tiles are 'encaustic tiles' – unique because their decorative designs are inlaid patterns created when coloured clay is poured into deep moulds and fired, producing durable tiles.

The floor in St George's Hall was laid in 1852 and cost £2000. It is 140 feet (42m) long and 72 feet (22 m) wide.

* *

Mintons Ltd:

Minton & Co. Pottery and porcelain manufacturers. Their factory was founded in Stoke on Trent in 1793/6 by Thomas Minton (1765-1836), who was succeeded on his death by his son Herbert Minton (1793-1858). The factory traded under various styles until 1845 when Minton & Co. was adopted. In 1868 the firm split into two parts, one for tiles only, the other for china (though it also made tiles). From c1873 the china works was known as Mintons. The two names, Minton & Co. and Mintons, are often used indiscriminately.

There were a number of further changes leading to different names for the different parts of the business. In 1845 the tile business became a separate department, trading as Minton

& Co. for encaustic or inlaid tiles which were mostly floor tiles, and as Minton, Hollins and Co. for oriented or majolica wall tiles. After Herbert Minton's death in 1858, the tile business was continued by Michael Daintry Hollins, who had become a partner in 1845, while the china business continued by Colin Minton Campbell, who had become a partner in 1849. Hollins and Campbell carried on the partnership, until 1868 when they split up, Hollins carrying on the title business and Campbell the china works, trading as Minton's China Works, which also produced tiles (though not Encaustic tiles) until 1918.

The company had worked on many public buildings and grand palaces as well as in simple domestic houses. The firm exhibited widely at trade shows and exhibitions throughout the world and examples of its exhibition displays are held at the '*Smithsonian Institution*' in Washington DC where the company had gained many prestigious awards.

Photograph of Herbert Minton (1793-1858)

On his death, Minton was succeeded by his son *Herbert Minton* 1793-1858 – who developed new production techniques and took the business into new fields, notably including decorative 'encaustic tile' making, through his association with leading architects and designers, including Augustus Pugin and it was said Prince Albert himself.

The glazed encaustic tiles at Stanbrook are actually the work of Robert Minton Taylor, the great master who only traded for a short time.

In 1869, Robert had set up a new tile factory, trading as Robert Minton Taylor, until he was bought out by Campbell in 1875 as the Campbell Brick & Tile Co. Both the Campbell Tile Co. and Minton, Hollins & Co. were absorbed by H & R Johnson-Richards in the 1960s.

Some examples of the splendid Minton tiles at Stanbrook Abbey: - JRH©

Examples of the use of 'Minton tiles' at Stanbrook Abbey to create this stunning effect (see colour plate): - JRH©

Example of the splendid architecture and the use of Minton tiles at Stanbrook: - courtesy of Neil Styles©

The Minton tiles are a splendid feature of the present hotel and create a spectacular image linked to the use of light in the long cloister corridors: - courtesy of Handpicked Hotels©

The fine St Benedict mural and the cloisters with their Minton tiles: courtesy of Handpicked Hotels©

Details from the St Benedict Mural show the Benedictine rules of 'work, study and prayer': - JRH

Dame Joanna Jamieson painted the mural after her solemn profession in 1961, for the St Benedict's cloister, beside the enclosure door. It was said that this painting was superimposed on an earlier mural named 'Superb'.

The young monk was modelled on Dame Joanna's brother.

In the mural is the illustration of a Raven, and there is an interesting reason for this. In one story Benedict was given poisoned bread by a priest who was jealous of him and his fame. Knowing that the bread was poisoned St Benedict called to the raven, who would come and feed from his hand, to take it away to a place where no one could eat it. The raven flew away with the poisoned bread in his beak and disposed of it, then returned to be given food from the saint.

The capitals in the Callow Great Hall were carved by *R. L. Boulton*, and six sit low above the choir stalls. They depict angels playing musical instruments, reflective of the Benedictine Rule which cites Psalm 137/8 *'In sight of the Angels I will sing to you.'*

Some of the beautifully carved, 'Boulton' angels and fruit and foliage capitals in the church and adjoining chapels: - JRH©

Richard Lockwood Boulton – c1832-1905 –

was an English sculptor who founded the firm Messrs R. L. Boulton & Sons. They were centred in Cheltenham and built monuments made of iron and stone in the United Kingdom. One of their finest works was the Neptune fountain in Cheltenham:

The Neptune Fountain made of Portland Stone in 1893 by a local sculptor R. L. Boulton. It depicts Neptune being drawn by seahorses

This carving shows the figures of St Mark and St Matthew to the right of the Chancel arch, at the corner between the choir and the chancel. Each evangelist carries his gospel inscribed with a significant text from the beginning: *Vox Clamantis* – 'A voice crying' for St Mark and *Liber Generationum* – 'The Book of Generations' for St Matthew

This scene is taken from the south side of the great chancel arch and from the deeply moulded foliage emerges the half-figure of Moses. Note the horns projecting from his head. According to the Vulgate and Douay versions of Exodus 34:29, his face reflects the glory of God in horns of dazzling light that forced him to wear a veil. He is carrying the tablets of the Law and a veil

Boulton was also responsible for the series of carved heads around the abbey, representing many different benefactors and people who had represented the Church throughout history. Here are examples of some of them:

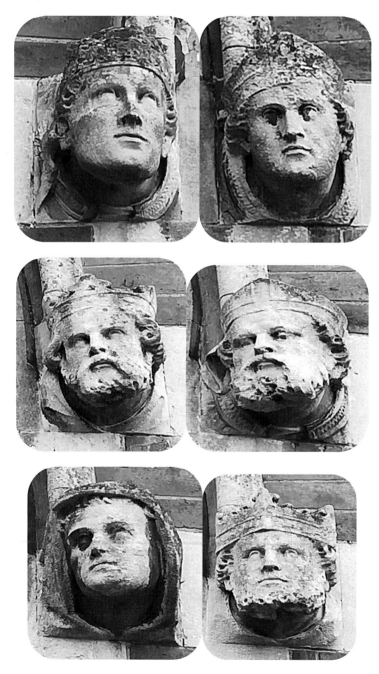

The fine angel carvings at the entrance to the Great Hall (see page 9 of Chapter 2). These angel dripstones and the moulded arch date from 1871 were added when the Sacristy block was built between 1898 and 1900: - JRH

The Modern Cloisters

The modern cloisters were designed by Martin Fisher, a Bath architect in 1962-63. The style at the time was in the same vein as Coventry Cathedral and other modernist church architecture of the late 50s and early 1960s. Here at Stanbrook the result was not wholly successful, although the cloister serves its utilitarian function of linking the various buildings on the site. At the junction between the two ranges there is a curious top-lit semi-chapel area, although this has never functioned as such.

The top-lit junction is a replica of the turret and 'fleche', or little steeple, crowning the (Benedictine) Abbey church of St Benoit-sur-Loire, Fleury, in France. It gave prominence to a statue of St Joseph (now at Stanbrook Abbey, Wass), patron of building and household matters

The modern cloisters with the Madonna statue (added since the community's move to North Yorkshire) at the far end: - JRH

The superb 'Boulton' carved heads of a King and Queen leading to St Anne's: - JRH

St Anne's Hall

St Anne's Hall is approached via the '*Via Crucis cloister,*' which also connects the former west entrance of the Callow Great Hall.

One of the fine stained glass windows in the Via Crucis which help to create the spectacular effects of light and shade in this particular passageway. People walking here at dusk have occasionally seen a faint outline of a figure coming towards them, but slightly suspended above the previous floor of the passage

The Via Crucis passageway leading towards the former entrance of the church, now the Callow Great Hall, (The former entrance was to the church itself (the choir), not to a chapel.):- JRH & Sister Philippa of Stanbrook©

The splendid mural covering the wall which was once the west entrance to the Church was painted by a Stanbrook Nun, Dame Werburg Welch. On either side are the carved 'Boulton' stoups- they contained holy water to make the sign of the cross on entering the church: - JRH©

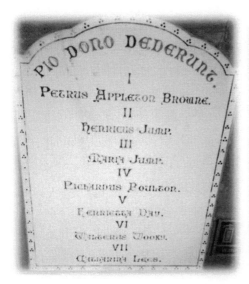
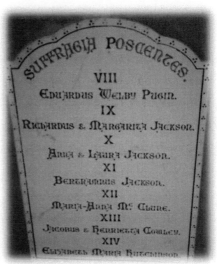

PIO DONO DEDERUNT.

I
PETRUS APPLETON BROWNE.
II
HENRICUS JUMP.
III
MARIA JUMP.
IV
RICHARDUS POULTON.
V
HENRIETTA DAY.
VI
WILHELMUS WOOKE.
VII
CATHARINA LEES.

SUFFRAGIA POSCENTES.

VIII
EDUARDUS WELBY PUGIN.
IX
RICHARDUS & MARGARITA JACKSON.
X
ANNA & LAURA JACKSON.
XI
BERTRAMUS JACKSON.
XII
MARIA-ANNA M^c CLARE.
XIII
JACOBUS & HENRIETTA COMLEY.
XIV
ELIZABETA MARIA HUTCHINSON.

The two plaques at the start of the Via Crucis passageway which are asking for prayers for the fourteen benefactors. Notice the names of Edward Welby Pugin (Number 8) and Richard Boulton (Number 4)

Along this cloister are fourteen 'stations of the cross' carved by R. L. Boulton. From right to left from the old entrance to the chapel - they include the following:

Jesus accepts his cross & Pilate condemns Jesus to die: - JRH

Jesus falls for the first time & Jesus meets his mother, Mary: - JRH

Simon helps to carry the Cross & Veronica wipes the face of Jesus: - JRH

Jesus falls for the second time & Jesus meets the three women from Jerusalem: - JRH

Jesus falls for the third time & Jesus is stripped of his clothes: - JRH

Jesus is nailed to the cross & Jesus dies on the cross: - JRH

Jesus is taken down from the cross & Jesus is placed in the tomb: - JRH

The Stations of the Cross or the Way of the Cross, also known as 'Way of Sorrows' or 'Via Crucis'.

These refer to a series of images found in many Catholic churches, depicting Jesus Christ on the day of his crucifixion and accompanying prayers. The stations grew out of imitations of *'Via Dolorosa'* in Jerusalem which is believed to be the actual path that Jesus walked holding the cross of his crucifixion to Mount Calvary.

The object of the stations is to help the Christian faithful to make a spiritual pilgrimage through contemplation of the Passion of Christ. It has become one of the most popular devotions and the stations can be found in churches of many different Christian denominations, including Anglican, Lutheran, and Methodist as well as most notably in Roman Catholic churches.

As at Stanbrook, the carved stone figures are in a series of 14 and the faithful travel from image to image, in order to stop at each station to say a selected prayer and reflect. This can be achieved individually or in a procession, mostly commonly taking place at Lent, especially on Good Friday, in a spirit of reparation for the suffering and insults Jesus endured during his passion. (source: Wikipedia)

The passageway of the 'Via Crucis' with the magnificent 'Minton floor tiles' and the sunlight coming through the stained glass windows: - JRH ©(see colour plate)

This beautifully carved crucifix is now sited in the Via Crucis passageway, but was moved from The Thompson Dining Room. It was said by the workmen who were moving this figure, that for a while it had been propped up on the wall ready to be put in place, and they felt it for a moment tremble with emotion. The INRI is translated as 'Jesus of Nazareth, King of the Jews' & SITIO as 'I Thirst.' : -JRH©

This splendid crucifix which dates from 1939 was designed by Dom Ephrem Seddon, a monk from Downside and assistant chaplain at Stanbrook. The figure was carved by a German woodcarver living in the Italian Tyrol, and the Cross itself was supplied by Robert Thompson of Kilburn, Yorkshire.

Detail from the face of Christ from the splendid crucifix in the Via Crucis: - JRH©

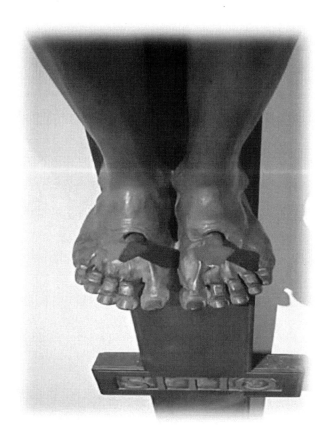

Details from the Via Crucis: - JRH (see colour plates)

The mural at the other end of the Via Crucis, which depicts the Crucifixion, was painted by a Stanbrook nun, Dame Werburg Welch: - JRH©

The early set of seven scenes was usually numbers 2, 3, 4, 6, 7, 11, and 14 from the list below. The standard set from the 17th to 20th centuries has consisted of 14 pictures or sculptures depicting the following scenes:

1. Pilate condemns Jesus to die
2. Jesus accepts his cross
3. Jesus falls for the first time
4. Jesus meets his mother, Mary
5. Simon helps carry the cross
6. Veronica wipes the face of Jesus
7. Jesus falls for the second time
8. Jesus meets the three women of Jerusalem
9. Jesus falls for the third time
10. Jesus is stripped of his clothes
11. Jesus is nailed to the cross
12. Jesus dies on the cross
13. Jesus is taken down from the cross
14. Jesus is placed in the tomb

Although not traditionally part of the Stations, the Resurrection of Jesus is, in very rare instances, included as a fifteenth station.

Out of the fourteen traditional Stations of the Cross, only eight have clear scriptural foundation. Stations 3, 4, 6, 7, and 9 are not specifically attested to in the gospels (in particular, no evidence exists of station 6 ever being known before medieval times) and Station 13 (representing Jesus's body being taken down off the cross and laid in the arms of his mother Mary) seems to embellish the gospels' record, which states that Joseph of Arimathea took Jesus down from the cross and buried him. To provide a version of this devotion more closely aligned with the biblical accounts, Pope John Paul II introduced a new form of devotion, called the Scriptural Way of the Cross on Good Friday 1991. He celebrated that form many times but not exclusively at the Colosseum in Rome.

In 2007, Pope Benedict XVI approved an overlapping but distinct set of stations for meditation and public celebration; they follow this sequence:

1. Jesus in the Garden of Gethsemane;
2. Jesus is betrayed by Judas and arrested;
3. Jesus is condemned by the Sanhedrin;
4. Jesus is denied by Peter;
5. Jesus is judged by Pilate;
6. Jesus is scourged and crowned with thorns;
7. Jesus takes up his cross;
8. Jesus is helped by Simon of Cyrene to carry his cross;
9. Jesus meets the women of Jerusalem;
10. Jesus is crucified;
11. Jesus promises his kingdom to the repentant thief;

12. Jesus entrusts Mary and John to each other;
13. Jesus dies on the cross; and
14. Jesus is laid in the tomb.

See: https://en.wikipedia.org/wiki/Wikipedia: Resusing-Wikipedia-content.

* *

St Anne's Hall was part of the original expansion by Charles Day in 1838. Day was a Worcester architect. Charles Day was the brother of Dame Justine Day of Stanbrook. He was responsible for the building of the small school block, later known as 'The Old House.'

The school closed in 1918. The lower part became the Bede Library, bathroom, Publications Room for the Abbey Press and Loom Room (for the weaving of the vestments and religious habits). From 1935-86 the upper part served as a noviciate, then as music practice and craft rooms.

W. H. Wood's watercolour of the west side of the chapel dated 1868, showing the original limewash or stucco finish. The schoolchildren are playing in the foreground: I am grateful to Sister Philippa Edwards and Sister Margaret Truran for information and this picture from the Stanbrook Abbey Archives©

A pre- 1898 view of the old monastery buildings showing some nuns walking around the formal gardens that, by this date, had been fully enclosed. In the middle are Abbess Placida Duggan (Abbess 1862-1868) and Dame Scholastica Gregson (Abbess 1846-1862 and 1868-1872) who are wearing cowls for the formal pose: cowls are not usually worn for work in the garden! - Grateful thanks to Sister Philippa Edwards and Sister Margaret Truran for information and this photograph from the Stanbrook Abbey Archives©

Charles Day – Worcester Architect

Charles Day (his son, also an architect was named Charles as well, which creates some confusion). The County Architect was also responsible for the Shire Hall in Worcester, which was built between 1834 and 1835 to Charles's design. He decided to emulate the Greek revival style favoured by *'Smirke'* and faced his building with a portico of six fluted Ionic columns. Worcester's secular concerts remained at the College Hall in the Cathedral for almost half a century more, until a fine organ by Nicholson (the same company who placed the present organ in Callow Great Hall) was installed in the Shire Hall. The change was made in 1884 in time for Dvorak's visit to Worcester, but surprisingly, no organ works were included in the secular concert programmes for that year.

College Hall in Worcester Cathedral 'Courtesy of the Dean and Chapter of Worcester Cathedral©

Charles Day's splendid Greek Revival style 'Shire Hall' with the Thomas Brock statue of Queen Victoria in front

The secular evening concerts, which had been such a popular feature of the eighteenth-century Music Meetings, continued on a regular basis until 1870. The balls which followed these concerts were gradually reduced to one only on the last night, until, as part of the 'call to seriousness' they were dropped altogether in 1874.

Charles Day also designed St Francis Xavier Church in Hereford. The foundation stone was laid on the 19th September 1837 and Queen Victoria sent her personal representation to the ceremony. Charles Day also designed St Edmund's Church in Bury for the Jesuits. The building construction cost over £16,000. It was opened on the 7th August 1839, before the restoration of the English Catholic hierarchy in 1850, and because of this the church has no windows.

St Francis Xavier's Church in Hereford

St Edmund's Church in Bury

In the Worcester Berrow's Journal for the 30ᵗ May 1833 is mentioned the following:

'On Saturday 25ᵗ, aged 60, Charles Day of Hawford Lodge, near this City.'

Hawford Lodge on the outskirts of the City of Worcester adjoining the modern A449: - JRH

_____

St Anne's Hall was used as the church of the abbey before the Callow Great Hall was completed. This was always a chapel, not a church.

The passageway with its fine 'Minton' tiles leading to St Anne's Hall & one of the early printing presses from Stanbrook: - JRH©

The flagstoned doorway leading into St Anne's Hall: - JRH©

The original Chapel in St Anne's Hall is used today in the hotel as a separate dining room or conference room. The windows are placed high up in the walls to prevent anyone looking through from outside and seeing a Catholic service taking place but also to prevent the praying nuns from being distracted from their prayers by the view!: - JRH©

Two early photographs of the St Anne's Chapel before the main Chapel was built

The enormous painting in the Italian style showing the 'Deposition' when Christ was taken down from the cross after his crucifixion. It was painted in 1832 by F. G. Gainsford and copied from Ribera's Proginal composition, now in the Certosa di San Martino, Naples

A reredos is an altarpiece, or an ornamental screen of the decoration behind the altar in a church, depicting religious iconography or images. In French and sometimes in English, this is called a *retable*; in Spanish *retablo.* It can be made of stone, wood, metal or even ivory, or with a combination of materials. The images may be painted, carved, gilded, composed of mosaics and/ or imbedded with niches for statues. Sometimes a tapestry is used or other fabric such as silk or velvet.

This picture was originally the reredos in a Chapel in Bath (opened in 1809 from a converted theatre in Orchard Street, Bath). This Chapel was replaced by Harrison's neo-gothic church in 1863, which is still standing. It is believed that Fr Laurence Shepherd (a chaplain and major benefactor of Stanbrook Abbey) worked closely with E. W. Pugin on the design and building of the Abbey. Fr Shepherd, who worked in Bath between 1855 and 1859 obtained the picture when the old chapel was closing and gave it to Stanbrook.

St Anne's Hall was used as a place of worship from 1838-1871, and there were benches for the children when they came to Mass. After 1871 it served as the Chapter house (the place for formal meetings of the monastic community) for the nuns, and at the end of the twentieth century as part of the library.

The summer house or 'alcove' was part of the playground for the children of the school here at the abbey. It was surrounded by a large variety of trees and shrubs. Many of these had become overgrown and had to be chopped down when the hotel took over. This brick summer house was part of the playground for the children of the school and there is a story that one of the stone balls on the top had to be replaced so a football was used and coated with cement! – photograph is courtesy of Neil Styles©

c1874 photograph of the summer house with a gathering of schoolchildren in the foreground and the statue of the Madonna is shown in the centre which survived until the 1960s: courtesy of the Stanbrook Abbey Archives©

Opposite the summer house and playground today, can be seen these two charming statues of the Virgin and Child and a small angel: - JRH

The hinges for the doors in the schoolroom and the ancient fire escape, which involved a pulley wheel which was secured while one shoulder belt let one person down, and the other strap came back up for the second person – very slow and probably not very efficient! – JRH©

One of the splendid windows in St Anne's Hall: - courtesy of Neil Styles Photographer©

After the main Abbey buildings had been completed, the St Anne's Hall became a huge library storage area. It has been quoted that it was estimated before the nuns left Stanbrook that there would have been around half a million ecclesiastical texts stored in this and other storage rooms in the Abbey. One such room still exists and today is the *Library Bar*.

The Library Bar in the present hotel: - JRH & Handpicked Hotels©

Bride's Manor:

This was the original Georgian house on the site. During the Stanbrook time as an Abbey, this was the presbytery where the priests would stay away from the main Abbey complex itself. It is connected to the Callow Great Hall by a private cloister, to allow the priests to enter the church separately to the nuns.

Today it is where guests can hire a separate set of accommodation a little apart from the main hotel. Here a wedding party can be accommodated and stay over for a few days with all the facilities they need.

Bride's Manor at Stanbrook Abbey Hotel

Bride's Manor and the drawing room at Bride's Manor: - courtesy of Handpicked Hotels©

The Bell Tower:

The Bell Tower can be accessed from the 'Via Crucis' passageway, just behind the former west entrance to the Callow Great Hall. The tower is 40 metres tall and contains 140 steps leading to a stunning view of the Abbey grounds and gardens as well as the surrounding Worcestershire countryside.

The Bell Tower at Stanbrook Abbey today. - JRH©

The bell tower in its distinctive red and white stone with various figures carved at the corners. One of the figures has worn and recently fallen. This would have been St Michael, resting on his sword, facing west. Boulton supplied two large statues; the other was King David, facing south

The Church Tower from the Garden of Remembrance with this fine statue of King David playing his harp: - JRH

The bells in the belfry of the tower and the seat at the top of the tower commanding splendid views of the surrounding countryside: - JRH©

One of the spectacular views from the top of the Bell Tower: - JRH©

Views from the top of the Bell Tower (see colour plates): - JRH©

The Garden of Remembrance:

The Garden of Remembrance was previously the Abbey Cemetery. Today the gardens are planted with grass and lavender and make a quiet, reflective area; it is a sacred and tranquil spot and the burial site for 141 nuns. The plaques which were originally attached to a wooden cross are now placed on the adjoining brick wall and make for some interesting reading.

Examples of some of the plaques from the Garden of Remembrance: - JRH©

The Crucifix in the Garden of Remembrance, a reminder of this sacred part of the Abbey: -
JRH©(see colour plate)

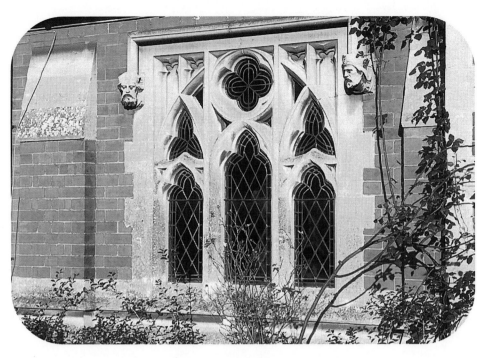

One of the fine carved windows overlooking the Garden of Remembrance with the 'Boulton' figure heads: - JRH

The carving of a crouching winged dragon on the roofline in the 'Garden of Remembrance'

Graves of famous figures (In the cemetery outside the church)

- **Dame Laurentia McLachlan**, writer, expert on Gregorian Chant and friend of G. Bernard Shaw. There are a play, a book, and a BBC film about her: all translated into several languages. *Entry in the Oxford Dictionary of National Biography, 2004.*

- **Dame Werburg Welch**, artist; her designs and woodcarvings can be found in different parts of the United Kingdom.

- **Dame Hildelith Cumming**, concert pianist, writer, letterpress printer. The Stanbrook Abbey Press, the oldest private press in the country, acquired an international reputation under Dame Hildelith – in 1988 a course of postgraduate studies in Church music was set up at the Royal Academy of Music as a result of her efforts.

- **Dame Felicitas Corrigan**, writer of numerous books, proponent of Gregorian Chant and church music advisor, and friend of Siegfried Sassoon and Alec Guinness. Her death in October 2003 attracted obituaries in all the main newspapers and 'The Economist'.

- **Dame Beatrice Brown**, church music adviser, sculptress and writer. Her sculpture of Abbess Gertrude's tomb in the Holy Thorn Chapel attracted attention in 1901, including an article in London's 'Daily Chronicle'. Her translations of St Teresa of Avila have remained in print for almost half a century.

- **Abbess Elizabeth Sumner**. Obituaries appeared in *The Times* and *The Independent,* in 1999.

- **Dame Brigid Allen**, a major figure in Patrick Benham's *The Avalonians (1993).* Her role in discoveries at Glastonbury merited attention in a recent doctoral thesis.

Another notable nun from Stanbrook Abbey is Mary O'Hara the Irish soprano and harpist from County Sligo. Mary achieved fame on both sides of the Atlantic in the late 1950s and early 60s. Her recordings from that time influenced a generation of Irish female singers.

Mary was introduced to the American poet Richard Selig by the Irish poet Thomas Kinsella and they married in 1956. She moved to the United States with him. Selig died of Hodgkin's disease just 15 months after their marriage. Mary was devastated but continued to tour and record for the next four years.

In 1962 she became a Benedictine nun at Stanbrook Abbey, where she stayed for 12 years. Her wedding band was melted down and made into a ring to celebrate her profession of solemn vows as a full member of the Benedictine Order in 1967.

Mary's initial speedy rise to fame was repeated in 1974 when she left Stanbrook for the sake of her health and found that her musical reputation had grown during the time she had spent in Stanbrook, and returned to performing. In a matter of months, she became one of the biggest international recording stars to come out of Ireland.

Solemn Profession Day, Stanbrook 1967. Mary in 'full battledress', holding snowdrops that her father had sent in that morning (This is one of the rare photographs taken of Mary as a Benedictine: - acknowledgement to Mary O'Hara's autobiography 'The Scent of Roses.'

(left to right) Dames Philippa Edwards, Rosemary Davies, and Raphael Foster of Stanbrook Abbey: courtesy of Sister Philippa Edwards and Mary O' Hara 'The Scent of the Roses.'©

The title of her autobiography, 'The Scent of the Roses, was taken from one of her favourite songs by the Irish poet Thomas Moore. Her other books include 'Celebration of Love' and the coffee table book 'A Song for Ireland.'

Her autobiography has a fascinating chapter on 'Stanbrook Abbey' and the 12 years she spent here. On entering the Abbey she writes with emotion of the parting with her father:

'After breakfast I went with the Lady Abbess to the parlour to see my father. Clearly, it was a shock to him that I was already well and truly 'inside' with a double grill dividing us. I think he expected me to be able to stroll outside in the garden with him. For a while the three of us chatted briefly and cheerfully together, which I think helped him. Soon it was time to go. We exchanged goodbyes through the grille and he departed, making a valiant effort to hide his emotions. He had known from the time he got news of Richard's death that I'd wanted and intended to enter a monastery, but he didn't believe I ever would.'

One of the most moving quotations in her book reveals something of her devotion to her faith and her calling as a nun in the Benedictine Order:

'I believed that I had a call to the monastic life, but I was fully prepared to leave this to the judgement of my superiors. I was fully aware that my first five years in the monastery must be a period of probation. Richard's death and the circumstances surrounding it had made me detached from earthly things. It had caused me to realize with unusual clarity how brief and fleeting this life is – whether one lives to be twenty-seven (as Richard did) or ninety-seven. If you are a Christian, then the death of someone you love more than life itself can be a tremendous eye-opener, if you have been with them through their dying. You see things and events in their proper perspective, as they really are.'

Mary gives us an interesting insight into life within the walls of Stanbrook Abbey for a nun in an enclosed order, when entering one would expect to spend the rest of one's life here within the enclosure:

'Once a year every able-bodied member of the community participated in harvesting the potatoes. A farmer came up with a special potato-digging machine and the nuns lined up along the drills putting the potatoes into sacks. During my early days as a postulant, one of my jobs was to go round with a tin picking slugs off the winter lettuce. I gave myself the title 'Inspector of Slugs.' Another congenial chore was looking after the Muscovy ducks that lived on the pond with the moorhens. In the spring and summer it was very pleasurable working out of doors in the morning, sometimes feeding the ducks. In summertime individuals often prayed outside between 5.30 and 6.25am. Come spring and I was sent to sow seed. I was reminded of the parable of the sower in the Gospel. I punned in my letter to my father that I was still broadcasting.'

'After my time in the kitchens, I was appointed First Portress for two consecutive years. This was a considerably less strenuous job than of Second Cook. It involved fetching nuns when they were wanted on the phone or in the parlour, and letting such people as had come inside the inclosure in and out. For those two years my afternoon work period was spent in the orchards. In wintertime it was generally light work involving ladders and secateurs. Scything in the summer months and making compost heaps called for more muscle. We had a few compost heaps located around the enclosure and for easier identification I gave them names such as Etna and Vesuvius, after various volcanoes. There were times when I climbed apple trees that were quite tall, and the delight of the operation made me wonder why I waited till I was thirty before attempting to climb trees.'

In due course and after spending 12 years in the community at Stanbrook, Mary's health had deteriorated so much, that it was decided that it was best she left the monastery and returned to normal life outside the community, not an easy task after living in the enclosed abbey for so long.

'It was a Saturday afternoon. October 12th 1974 that I said goodbye to Stanbrook physically depleted. I felt spiritually invigorated and incalculably enriched. I knew the road back to full vitality and health would not be easy, but with God's help I was prepared for whatever the future might hold.'

* *

The Sacristy Buildings on the East Side

The East side of the Abbey with its decorative finials and decorated stone windows contrasting with the deep red brick, so typical of the Pugin style: - JRH

The Sacristy comprises a grouping of elements on the east end of the church and a major wing projecting to the east at the south end of the east wing of the late 19th century monastery. The main wing has a gable end with a sculptural niche as its centrepiece. To the left of this is a further range of rooms (containing the boys' sacristy on the ground floor) which has a parapeted roof.

The parapet on the Sacristy roof and the finely carved figure of the crowned Virgin and Child, the work of Boulton of Cheltenham, was erected in 1886

The decorative carved niche with the fine statue of the crowned Madonna and Child: - JRH

The Groom's Room

This was once the *Sacristy* (a room in a church where a priest prepares for a service and where vestments and articles of worship are kept). Here the visiting clergy prepared and robed for the services and the vestments were also kept here. The main sacristy was within the enclosure, whereas the extern sacristy was not. So the sacristan, a fully enclosed nun, would prepare the correct vestments, a skilled business, and send them through to the extern sacristy, where the extern nuns would take them out of the drawer for the celebrant.

The wooden panelling in the Groom's Room and the wooden drawer containing the vestments of the visiting celebrant. The two sides of the sacristy that part within the enclosure and the part that was not: -JRH©

This room was once one of several visitors' parlours. The nuns at Stanbrook were enclosed; visitors could not enter inside the enclosure but were welcomed inside the parlours, where the nuns would come and meet them. Hospitality is an important strand in the life of the Benedictine nuns; 'guests are never lacking in a monastery,' as the Rule of St Benedict declares. The present day Piano Bar was formerly the Large Parlour where all the community could greet and meet guests. A counter and grille ran across the room. In 1971 the grille was removed, and the counter in the 1980s.

The Piano Bar at the present hotel: - courtesy of Handpicked Hotels©

The iron grills on the front door of the monastery

On the outside door close to the *'Postern Gate'* is a bell and list of those handymen such as the gardener or other workmen who were allowed inside the Abbey to do their work. Also marked is the Abbey car and van, presumably used to collect provisions or make journeys. This simple system shows if the car or person is 'in' or 'out'.

Thompson Hall:

Thompson Hall is named after Robert Thompson who carved fine oak fittings for this the 'refectory' of the abbey during the nuns' occupation and is today one of the main banqueting and function rooms in the hotel. The fine fittings were placed in various stages from 1926 to 1940, including a panelled screen at the west end and a pulpit to the east, all under the direction of the architect J. Arnold Crush.

Robert (Mouseman) Thompson – 7th May 1876-8th December 1955 – was a British furniture maker and designer who lived in Kilburn, North Yorkshire. Thompson set up a woodcarving business manufacturing oak furniture which always features a carved mouse on every piece.

The 'Thompson mouse' carved on the pulpit stand in the Thompson Dining Room: - JRH©

It is claimed that the mouse motif came about accidentally in 1919 following a conversation which included the phrase 'being as poor as a church mouse' which took place between Thompson and one of his colleagues during the carving of a cornice for a screen. This conversation resulted in Thompson carving a mouse on many of his pieces.

Robert Thompson was part of the 1920s revival of craftsmanship, inspired by the 'Arts and Crafts movement' led by William Morris, John Ruskin and Thomas Carlyle. More specific to furniture making in this genre and era included Stanley Webb Davies of Windermere.

The workshop which is now being run by his descendants, includes a showroom and a 'Visitor Centre' and is located beside the Parish Church, which contains 'Mouseman' pews, fittings and other furniture. The company is today known as 'Robert Thompson's Craftsmen Ltd – The Mouseman of Kilburn.'

Much of the furniture and fittings at Ampleforth College come from the Thompson workshop.

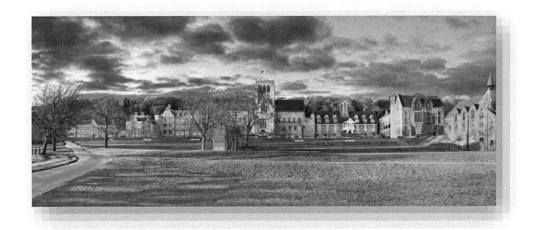

Ampleforth in North Yorkshire

In the Thompson Hall at Stanbrook there can be seen hand carved wooden panelling and at the other end of the room a raised stage with a mounted lectern that was made under the direction of the architect J. Arnold Crush.

The raised stage with mounted lectern at Stanbrook Abbey: JRH©

The inscription on the canopy bears the text of a piece of Gregorian chant in the Worcester Antiphoner: 'Christus Vincit, Christus Regnat, Christus Imperat' - 'Christ Conquers, Christ Reigns, Christ Governs (with imperial power)' - JRH

The Worcester Antiphoner is a highly important manuscript in the Worcester Cathedral Library containing the chants sung by the Benedictine monks in Worcester in the Middle Ages. Abbess Laurentia McLachlan, who installed the pulpit in 1933, has produced a facsimile edition of the manuscript, with a major commentary.

The rose in the corner near the wall symbolizes *Our Lady of Consolation*, patroness of the community.

The three carved panels on the stage and lectern stand in the Thompson Dining Room: JRH

The front of the pulpit displays the coats of arms of the community's ecclesiastical benefactors at Cambrai, where the community was founded in exile:

1. Dom Rudesind Barlow – President of the Benedictine Congregation. He was responsible for the foundation of the monastery in 1623.
2. Urban VIII, Pope from 1623-1644. In 1638 he confirmed the monastery of the exiled English Benedictine nuns at Cambrai, in the wake earlier that year of the outright gift of their buildings. The heraldic arms display the bees of the Barberini family, to which Urban VIII belonged.
3. Archbishop Vanderburg of Cambrai – he gave a warm welcome to the new monastery and its nine foundresses.

The carved oak panel from the Thompson Dining Room: JRH©

The crucifix (now in the Via Crucis) and the panelling behind the abbatial table (1940: Thompson) were a belated silver jubilee present from Dame Martha van Overbeke's family.

Around the walls are heraldic shields relating to the key figures in the Benedictine Nuns' past:
JRH©

The shields include those of Lady Cecilia Heywood who was blessed as abbess in November 1897 and was the twentieth in succession from the year 1629 when the community was first created. Frances Watson, Margaret Vavasour, Catherine Gascoigne and Anne Morgan were some of the nuns who left England. Cresacre More financed the foundations. Abbess Lady Gertrude L. d'Aurillac Dubois was the abbess before Lady Cecilia Heywood and finally there was the shield of Abbess Elizabeth Summer. These carved heraldic shields were an important part of the history and depict key personalities and also show us the importance of this particular room where the nuns would have congregated for their meals.

The magnificent carved oak ceiling showing the position of the Heraldic shields: - JRH©

A postcard (C6469) showing the original Stanbrook Abbey Refectory: - courtesy of Stanbrook Abbey Archives©

The Benedictine nuns were enclosed; therefore guests could not enter the enclosure. But the nuns regularly met guests, including priests, in the parlours. A grille running across the parlours separated nuns from guests, but it did not stop them from seeing each other or exchanging books etc. The parlours were not built to accommodate guests; for this there was a guest house, a separate building, down the drive.

A fine conference room at the present hotel: - courtesy of Handpicked Hotels©

These were located in the east wing of the present abbey on the ground floor and were rooms that contained dividing grills that marked the line of the convent enclosure, and these were accessed by a separate corridor. There was a large parlour which was used when the whole community met guests. This was built at the north end of the abbey.

The East wing of the Abbey. The figure in the niche at the corner between the east and north wings of the abbey is a statue of St Peter, 6' 2", the work of Boulton, Cheltenham. It arrived on the 7th May 1886 with a statue of Our Lady & Child, which was placed on the east wing of the sacristy: - JRH

In the two Boulton statues St Peter is seen blessing with his right hand and holding a key in his left. Vine and oak leaves are carved on the pedestal. The statue of Our Lady and child are shown crowned and with a sceptre in her left hand.

Both statues were the gift of Sister Johanna Manning, novice and niece of Cardinal Manning and the noviciate companion of Dame Laurentia McLachlan.

The East Entrance for visitors and the ornate iron doorbell pull: - JRH

The carved coat of arms on the East side of the Abbey: - JRH

The coat of arms records in gratitude that the side wing jutting out from the east front was built between 1898 and 1900 thanks to the generosity of the Cary family. The arms (a pelican and three Tudor roses) are those of the Cary family. The motto of the family reads – *Ad mortem fidelis* which translated means 'faithful unto death.' Four of the Cary family were nuns at Stanbrook at this time.

This shows the corridor, known as the Priest's Cloister, that leads to the extern chapel of the church. This gave the chaplain an entrance separate from the monastery, and also separate from the public entrance to the church. In the extern chapel there was a marble altar, enabling priests to celebrate Mass privately. The grille separating this chapel from the sanctuary was not erected until 1971. The previous Hardman grille ran across the altar steps dividing the nuns' choir from the sanctuary; this was removed in 1971. In both instances the public and the nuns were separated.

The stunning Hardman stained glass window from 1870, in the public access area of the chapel, shows Christ with his favourite disciple St John: - JRH©

𝔖ister 𝕮harlotte's 𝕽estaurant – the 𝕮alefactory or 'warming room' of the 𝕬bbey

– The 'Sister Charlotte's' Restaurant in the present hotel was once the 'Calefactory' or 'warming room' of the Abbey. This was the common meeting room of the nuns of Stanbrook, where they would gather to warm themselves, particularly in the colder seasons and where they could pursue delicate work such as sewing or embroidery. It housed a communal fire (there is a fireplace at either end of the room) and in the earlier days of the convent it would have been one of the warmest rooms in the abbey. In the north wing, the corridors were heated with radiators and the rising air from the stone stairs well. Below in the infirmary there was also a fireplace.

In the east wing, there were fireplaces in the public rooms on the ground floors, two in the abbatial apartment, another in the guest cell and the linen room and other rooms. In August 1903 heating pipes were introduced into some of the cells, and eventually into all of them.

Sister Charlotte's Restaurant, once the 'Calefactory' of the Abbey and sited on the second floor of the Abbey. This is a large open room which must have taken some heating: - JRH©

The kitchen unit alongside the Calefactory at Stanbrook: - JRH

The 'Calefactory' was one of the most important rooms in the medieval monasteries of Western Europe. It had a communal fire which was kept alight so that the monks could warm themselves after long hours of study in the often draughty cloisters.

The Last Supper is a late 15th-century mural painting by Leonardo da Vinci housed by the refectory or 'calefactory' of the Convent of Santa Maria delle Grazie in Milan. It is one of the world's most recognizable paintings

The Cellars and Kitchens:

The kitchen, pantry and scullery conform to the original plan, today fitted with modern equipment. The cellars beneath the north range also retain their plan for the laundry rooms and the original bread oven made by Parker of Birmingham in the tiled backhouse.

Parker of Birmingham:

The extensive cellars at Stanbrook Abbey:-JRH©

The cast iron 'Parker' bread oven where the nuns on kitchen duty would prepare the dough for the bread. This would be placed early in the morning in the oven and then they would go for morning Mass. This was the first Mass and not long and so time to be back before the bread had baked. The longer solemn sung Mass followed later

One of the former storerooms in the kitchen area. In the modern hotel it is used as a small private dining room: - JRH

An electric pump in the courtyard outside the kitchen area, which was used for pumping water into the abbey laundry and kitchens: - JRH

An iron water pump and basin behind the kitchen area, used for a variety of purposes, such as the cleaning of tools of those nuns who had been gardening or working outside in the day: - JRH

Another small private dining area in the modern hotel, situated in the former wine cellar: - JRH

The fine Minton tiles being used here below ground, and the collection of wine and champagne bottles on display: - JRH

This splendid mural at the end of the underground passageway showing the maid pushing the dust behind the curtains! : - JRH

The snooker room for Hotel Guests: courtesy of Handpicked Hotels©

The snooker room and games room in the modern Stanbrook Abbey Hotel: - Handpicked Hotels©

Storage room and washbasin in the cellars of the Abbey

Slate shelves for storing food in this cold room

At the first floor level is the abbess's room and its anteroom, which retain their fireplaces and the linen room has its original cupboards and the linen presses lining the walls. The corridors to the top three floors are all centrally heated with radiators, but the cells have only pipes. Each cell has its original door with chamfered detailing. The circular inlets for the ventilation system are in situ as is the dumb waiter leading from the pantry to the first and third floors.

The 'Abbess Suite' and the 'Dame Suite' in the modern hotel: - JRH

The window and the fireplace in the Abbess's room: - JRH

One of the modern bedrooms, once one of the nun's cells: courtesy of Handpicked hotels©

One of the communal water taps along the upper floor corridors with the cells on either side and the niche with the carved Madonna: - JRH

There are various interesting staircases in the abbey, some carved in an elaborate 'arts and crafts' style.

This is a curious light well-like central slot with moulded arches and the carved Pugin staircase: - JRH©

Examples of some of the fine Pugin staircases at Stanbrook: - JRH

Example of one of the beautifully carved 'arts and crafts' style Pugin staircases at Stanbrook: - JRH

There are a variety of different guest bedrooms in the modern Stanbrook Hotel. These have been converted from the original nuns' bedrooms and other rooms in the original Abbey. Some were very small and narrow, and have been divided into a bedroom and an en suite taking two adjoining rooms. The result is an interesting combination of single, twin and double rooms.

Interesting original features have been incorporated into the modern hotel bedrooms: - courtesy of Handpicked Hotels©

This converted bedroom shows just how small the original nuns' rooms were, just the simple bed and a table and a chair, and maybe a small bookcase

* *

Stanbrook Abbey Hotel: - courtesy of Handpicked Hotels©

An aerial view of the Abbey and the splendid views from the Church tower: - JRH & Handpicked Hotels©

~ II ~

The Great Hall and former chapel of the Abbey of Stanbrook: - courtesy of Handpicked Hotels©

~ III ~

The splendid 'Clayton and Bell' stained glass window at the East end of the Great Hall: - JRH

~ IV ~

George's Bar in the modern hotel & one of the cloister passages showing the magnificent Minton tiles: - courtesy of Handpicked Hotels©

~ V ~

Mural of St Benedict with the Raven and the figures representing 'Work, Study & Prayer'

~ VI ~

One of the fine blood red stained glass windows in the Via Crucis Cloister and an example of the splendid 'Minton' tiles which can be found in the Abbey: - courtesy of Neil Styles©

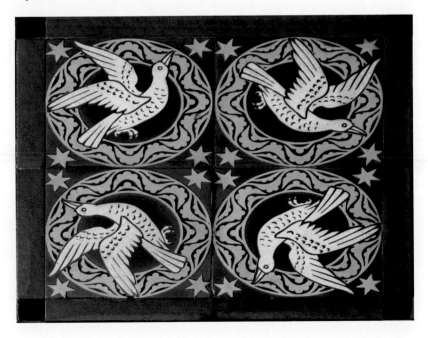

The entrance door into the Great Hall, the former Chapel with the ornate 'stoups' on either side: - courtesy of Neil Styles©

One of the fine 'Pugin' staircases at Stanbrook: - courtesy of Neil Styles©

~ IX ~

St Anne's Hall the former chapel to the abbey & the Thompson Dining Room the former refectory of the abbey: - courtesy of Handpicked Hotels©

Some examples of the bedrooms in the modern Stanbrook Hotel:- courtesy of Handpicked Hotels©

Former Parlour for the visitors to the Abbey, the mural in the cellar & collection of wine bottles

The stunning 'Hardman' West Window in the Great Hall at Stanbrook Abbey: - JRH©

~ XIII ~

Examples of the Boulton Carvings in Stanbrook Abbey

Examples of the 'Boulton' carvings from the Great Hall: - JRH

~ XV ~

The fine carvings on the choir stalls in the Great Hall: - JRH

~ XVI ~

The splendid and emotionally moving spiritual statue of Christ overlooking the Garden of Remembrance: - JRH©

The Via Crucis Cloister on a sunny autumn morning: - JRH©

~ XVIII ~

The magnificent crucifix from the 'Via Crucis' Cloister: - JRH

~ XIX ~

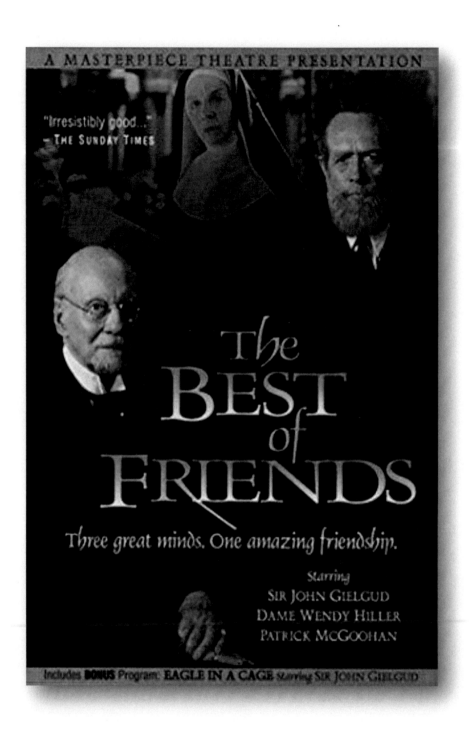

The Best of Friends poster

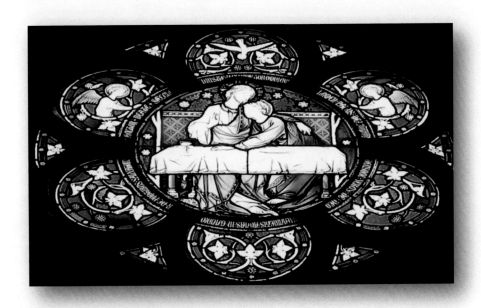

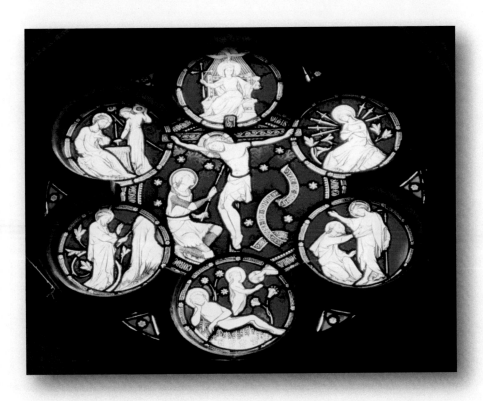

Two of the stunning 'Hardman' stained glass windows at Stanbrook: - JRH

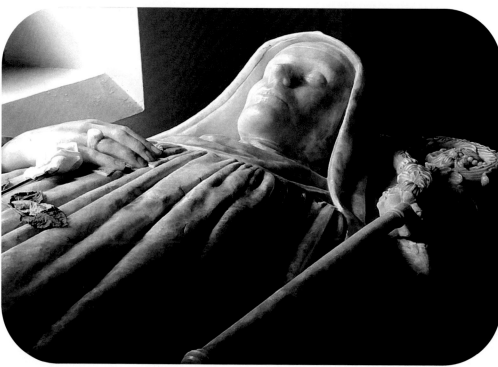

The tombs of Dom Laurence Shepherd (d. 1885) & Abbess Gertrude D'Aurillac Dubois (d. 1897)
in the Chapel of the Holy Thorn, Stanbrook: - JRH©

~ XXII ~

The use of white colour, the careful use of light and the stunning 'Minton Tiles' make this passageway incredibly beautiful: - JRH©

~ XXIII ~

Two of the cloister passageways display the magnificent 'Minton Tiles':- courtesy of Neil Styles©

The modern 'Stanbrook Abbey' at Wass, Yorkshire:- courtesy of the Stanbrook Community at Wass©

Postcard (C6469) Stanbrook Abbey Refectory

*Caravaggio 'The Crowning with Thorns' - 1603 & 'Christ Carrying the Cross' as portrayed
by El Greco, 1580*

~ XXVII ~

The Great Hall set out for a wedding & Stanbrook Abbey in the snow: - courtesy of Handpicked Hotels©

~ XXVIII ~

Stanbrook Abbey at Night & another Hardman and Co. Stained Glass window: - courtesy of the Stanbrook Abbey Hotel©

A Wedding Marque at Stanbrook Abbey and the interior lounge of Brides Manor: - courtesy of Handpicked Hotels©

~ XXX ~

The Games Room at Stanbrook Abbey: - courtesy of Handpicked Hotels©

The Library Lounge and Brides Manor: - courtesy of Handpicked Hotels©

Chapter Three: Stanbrook Abbey Printing Press

The John Rylands Library, Manchester, purchased a large collection of documents from the Stanbrook Abbey Press which included over 250 items.

The press was founded at Stanbrook in 1876 and was run by the religious community rather than by an individual or a partnership. It stood at the interface between book design and religious belief.

Famously the press was associated in the early part of the twentieth century with one of the great figures of English bibliography, *Sir Sydney Cockerell*. He in turn introduced the nuns to *Emery Walker* and *C. H. St John Hornby*.

Sir Sydney Cockerell – 1867- 1962

Sydney Cockerell – 1909: courtesy of The Fitzwilliam Museum – University of Cambridge©

Sir Sydney Carlyle Cockerell was an English museum curator and important collector. From 1908 to 1937 he was the director of the *Fitzwilliam Museum* in Cambridge. He initially started in life working as a clerk in his family coal business *George J. Cockerell & Co.* until he was inspired on meeting *John Ruskin* and his radical views. According to 'John Ruskin' by Tim Hilton (p816) he had sent Ruskin some seashells which he had collected. John Ruskin was interested and drew many examples of natural shapes from nature. At this time Cockerell had already met *William Morris* and become interested in the '*Arts and Crafts*' movement which was proving so popular at this time.

From 1891, Cockerell gained a more solid entry into intellectual circles, working for the *'Society for the Protection of Ancient Buildings.'* *Detmar Blow* the architect was his friend at this time. He acted as private secretary to *William Morris,* and became a major collector of 'Kelmscott Press' books; he was also secretary to *Wilfred Scawen Blunt;* and was *Thomas Hardy's* executor being highly respected in the society of the time.

From 1908 to 1937 he was the Director of the 'Fitzwilliam Museum' in Cambridge. He built up the Museum's collections of private press books and manuscripts including those from Stanbrook Abbey in Worcestershire. He collected drawings, paintings, ceramics and antiquities. It was he who secured the Museum's holdings of works by *William Blake* and bought its first Picasso print. He raised funds for building extensions, set up the first 'Friends' scheme in Britain and introduced Sunday opening.

The Fitzwilliam Museum in Cambridge- looking very much like the British Museum in London

Cockerell appears as one of a circle of three figures in the book by *Dame Felicitas Corrigan,* 'The Nun, the Infidel, and the Superman', with *Dame Laurentia McLachlan* from Stanbrook Abbey and *George Bernard Shaw.* It was later dramatized by Hugh Whitemore as 'The Best of Friends' and was produced on stage at the Hampstead Theatre in 2006 and on television in 1991.

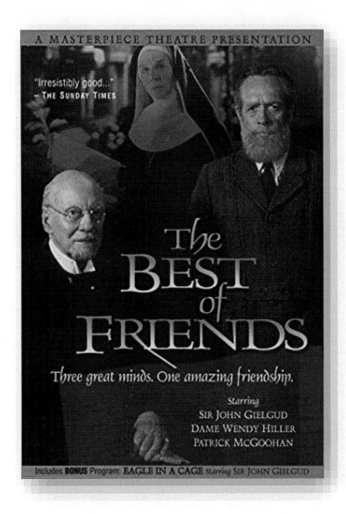

Poster for the theatre presentation of 'The Best of Friends' starring Sir John Gielgud, Dame Wendy Hiller and Patrick McGoohan

He was a leading figure in the revival of italic handwriting as an artistic craft and was particularly interested in the work being done using different fonts and styles at the *Stanbrook Printing Press* in Worcestershire.

Emery Walker: 1851-1933 – was an English engraver, photographer and printer who took an active role in many organisations that were at the heart of the 'Arts and Crafts' movement, including the *Art Workers Guild, the Society for the Protection of Ancient Buildings* and the *Arts and Crafts Exhibition Society.*

Emery Walker

(In Britain, **the Arts and Crafts Movement** flourished from about 1880. Inspired by the ideas of John Ruskin and William Morris, it advocated a revival of traditional handicrafts, a return to a simpler way of life and an improvement in the design of ordinary domestic objects.)

C. H. St John Hornby- 1867-1946 – was the founding partner in *W.H. Smith*, deputy vice-chairman of the NSPCC and the founder and owner of the *Ashendene Press.*

Hornby was born on the 25th June 1867 at Much Dewchurch in Herefordshire. He was the eldest son of the Reverend Charles Edward Hornby, then a curate and his wife Harriet. He was educated at Harrow and New College, Oxford, where he received a bachelor's degree in Classics.

New College Oxford

Harrow School

In 1892, Hornby was called to the bar, but his friend *Freddy Smith* (with whom he had spent a year from 1890-91 travelling the world) offered him a partnership in *W. H. Smith* the family business.

In 1900 Hornby met Emery Walker and Sydney Cockerell (then William Morris' secretary at the Kelmscott Press). Together they encouraged and instructed Hornby and helped with the devising of two typefaces for his own use, the *'Subiaco'* and the *'Ptolemy.'* He became interested as were his colleagues with the Stanbrook Abbey Press and contacted and worked with the Nuns at the abbey.

Hornby married *Cicely Rachel Emily Barclay*, the daughter of *Charles Barclay*, a director of the National Provincial Bank, and Charlotte Cassandra Cherry on 19th January 1898. They had homes at Shelley House, Chelsea, London and at Chantmarle in Dorset.

Shelley House on the Chelsea Embankment

Chantmarle Manor in Dorset

The Stanbrook Abbey Press enjoyed a golden age under the direction of Dame Hildelith Cumming, who was printer from 1955 until her death in 1991.

Dame Hildelith Cumming – 1909 – 1991 –

Dame Hildelith Cumming in 1976

Dame Hildelith Cumming was a British nun and musician who was born as *Barbara Theresa Cumming*. She was a convert to the Roman Catholic faith and became from 1955 the head printer at Stanbrook Abbey. She was responsible for earning the press a sterling reputation as an excellent and notable private press.

The Stanbrook Abbey Press by 1952 was in decline, even though it held the reputation for being the oldest private printing press in England. Under her leadership and encouragement the press flourished . *John Dreyfus* and the typographer *Jan van Krimpen* she also contacted for advice. She employed the services of Harry and Margaret Adams, both trained calligraphers. *Dame Felicitas Corrigan* worked in the press in her early years but she was important in making major contributions through her ideas, literary expertise and faultless proofreading.

With the support and encouragement of *Jan van Krimpen* and the English designer *John Dreyfus,* Dame Hildelith developed a distinctive Stanbrook style, which became famous for its use of characterful typefaces, expertly printed on fine handmade papers; the deployment of white spaces to allow texts to 'breathe', and liveliness through coloured inks, calligraphic decoration and fine bindings.

David Butcher, the press's bibliographer, summed up its achievement: '*Collectively the books published by the Press ... earn it a place as one of the world's major private presses... The books are an enduring testament to the Benedictine aim of employing human talents to the glory of God.*'

In 2007 the *John Rylands Library in Manchester* purchased a major collection of the Stanbrook Abbey Press's output, with the funding from the *Friends of John Rylands.*

The collection includes all but one of the thirty-nine major works published by the Press in the period 1956-90, (the missing item being the scarce *'Rituale Abbatum'* of 1963); thirty - four out of forty-three works printed at Stanbrook on behalf of others; seventeen of the attractive illuminated folders for which the Press was renowned; and scores of minor items, prospectuses, price lists and jobbing work.

Some items are particularly scarce, such as one of twenty special copies of *Siegfried Sassoon's* 'The Path to Peace' signed by the author and one of twenty specials of another major work, *Raissa Maritain's* 'Patriarch Tree.'

Copyright – Siegfried Sassoon
Printed in England at the
Stanbrook Abbey Press
Worcester

Raissa Maritain- 1883-1960 was a Russian born French poet and philosopher. She emigrated to France and studied at the Sorbonne, where she met the young Jacques Maritain, also a philosopher, whom she married in 1904. She was raised as a Jew but, following a period in which she considered herself an atheist, converted to Roman Catholicism with her husband in 1906

There are fourteen items not recorded in Butcher's bibliography, as well as many variants and trial pages. There are a few examples of the earlier output of the Stanbrook Press, from the late nineteenth and early twentieth centuries. Particularly significant is a handwritten and probably unique list of books printed between 1876 and 1962, with later annotations and additions by Dame Hildelith. There is also a handful of letters from Dame Hildelith to collectors. *(Thanks to the John Rylands Library in Manchester for this information)*

Stanbrook Abbey in Literature

Stanbrook Abbey as well as being the setting for the play '*The Best of Friends*' is also used as the inspiration for other books.

Iris Murdoch's novel, '*The Bell*' was published in 1958 and is set at *Imber Court*, a lay religious community situated close by an enclosed order of Benedictine nuns in Gloucestershire. The setting described in the novel is very similar to Stanbrook. The story follows the trials and tribulations of several characters in a lay community with a variety of problems. Throughout the novel the image of a butterfly is used as the symbol of the soul, and of wisdom.

Irish Murdoch's funny and also sad novel is about religion, the fight between good and evil and the terrible accidents of human frailty. A new bell is being installed in the nearby abbey and then the old bell, legendary symbol of religion and magic, is rediscovered.

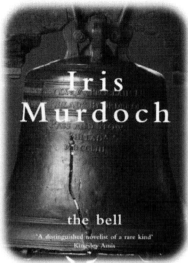

Iris Murdoch and her novel 'The Bell'

Rumer Godden's novel 'In this House of Brede' which was published in 1969 is considered to show an insightful portrait of religious life. The plot of the novel focuses on Philippa Talbot the protagonist, who is a highly successful professional woman who leaves her life among the London elite to join a cloistered Benedictine community at *Brede Abbey.* Stanbrook was undoubtedly the model for the abbey in the novel. Rumer Godden wrote the novel at Stanbrook with the help of Dame Felicitas Corrigan. A Panel of three nuns scrutinized the script. The plan of the ground and first floors of Brede Abbey, drawn by Dame Joanna Jamieson of Stanbrook, is based on Stanbrook Abbey.

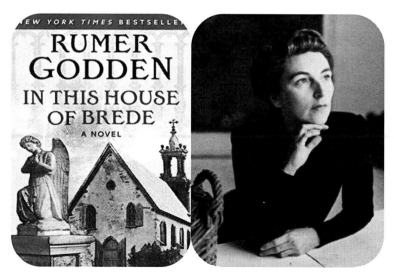

The novel 'In This House of Brede' and Rumer Godden in 1942

The plot, though is fictional. As Rumer wrote to Abbess Elizabeth Sumner of Stanbrook, 'The Difficulty has been that to make a story there has to be conflict and drama, which should both be alien to the life of a contemplative nun.' Those two elements were invented by Rumer.

Dame Laurentia McLachlan, OSB, nee Margaret McLachlan – 1866-1953 – was a Benedictine nun, who became one of the notable abbesses of Stanbrook Abbey and was an authority on church music.

She is portrayed in the Millennium window in Worcester Cathedral holding the 'Worcester Antiphoner.' She edited a facsimile of the manuscript, prefixed by a lengthy introduction. This was published as a volume in the *Paleographie Musicale* series issued by the Abbey of Solesmes. The Antiphoner is notable as it contains a unique and very rare sample of the music and services which took place in the Monastic Cathedral of Worcester during Medieval times.

The Worcester Antiphoner features liturgical text alongside early musical notation. Image copyright The Dean and Chapter of Worcester Cathedral (UK) ©

The Worcester Antiphoner: - Of particular note amongst the medieval manuscripts collection in the Worcester Cathedral Library is MS F.160, or the 'Worcester Antiphoner'. A liturgical service book dating from the 1230s, and written here at Worcester, it offers us a glimpse into what religious services in the medieval period would have been like. It contains an early form of musical notation (which can still be interpreted today), and it may well represent a tradition of sacred music that stretches back as far as the Anglo-Saxon period. What makes it especially significant is that it is the only book of

its kind that we know of from a Benedictine monastery to survive the Reformation in the United Kingdom.

McLachlan was born in Coatbridge, Lanarkshire, Scotland, the youngest of seven children of Henry McLachlan an accountant and his wife Mary. In 1884 aged 18 she joined the Benedictine Abbey at Stanbrook and was given the name of Dame Laurentia. In 1931 aged 65 she was elected the Abbess of Stanbrook. She had recently served the wider Benedictine community as a member of the commission set up to revise the constitutions of the houses of Benedictine nuns in the English Congregation. She was a pioneer in the restoration of the Gregorian chant in England, and a leading authority on music and medieval manuscripts, thanks especially to the loan of the Worcester Antiphoner by the Dean and Chapter of Worcester Cathedral. In 1934 her work was recognised by Pope Pius XI who bestowed on her the *Bene Merenti medal* for her contribution to Church music.

The Bene Merenti Medal of Pope Pius XI

Dame Laurentia died in 1953 at Stanbrook Abbey, having spent 70 of her 87 years in the enclosed monastery. She was one of five figures chosen to represent one thousand years of 'inspired Christian life' in Mark Cazalet's *Millennium Window* in the cloisters of Worcester Cathedral.

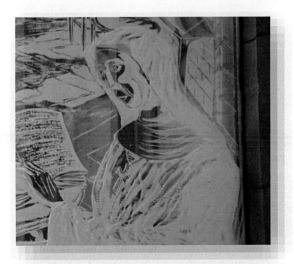

Mark Cazalet's 'Millennium Window' in the cloisters of Worcester Cathedral with a detail showing Dame Laurentia with the translated 'Worcester Antiphoner':-courtesy of Worcester Cathedral Dean and Chapter©

A 1988 stage play by Hugh Whitemore, 'The Best of Friends' (based on the book by Dame Felicitas Corrigan), provides a window on the friendship of McLachlan with Sir Sydney Cockerell and Bernard Shaw through adaptions from their letters and writings. McLachlan was first played by Rosemary Harris, then in the 2006 revival at the Hampstead Theatre, Patricia Routledge played the part.

THE **N**UN *THE* **I**NFIDEL AND THE **S**UPERMAN

The Remarkable Friendships
of Dame Laurentia McLachlan
with Sydney Cockerell,
Bernard Shaw, and Others

D. FELICITAS CORRIGAN

****

Chapter Four: The Gardens and Park

The grounds at Stanbrook Abbey are extensive. The abbey was pretty well self-sufficient and evidence of this still exists today. Much had to be cleared as the grounds had become overgrown, with the changes from when the abbey at its height. Much work had to be undertaken when *Clarenco* bought the property in 2010 in order to convert it into a first-class hotel. The grounds had become overgrown because of the changes from the abbey at its height looked after nearly 80 nuns, down to the time of the move in 2009, and the gradual winding down after the announcement in 2002 of the decision to move.

The present owners 'Handpicked Hotels' have also had an colossal task looking after the enormous grounds and bringing them to their present fine state. Unfortunately many beautiful trees had to be felled and shrubs which had grown to an enormous height had to be cut back so many changes to the landscaping of the buildings took place.

One notable area was the nuns' graveyard, and it is easy to forget that when postulants entered the noviciate, they were expected to spend the rest of their lives within its walls and eventually be buried here. When the nuns left in 2009, the cemetery outside the church and in use from 1878 was in good order.

The new owners faced with the maintenance of the cemetery, asked for the headstones to be removed. The ground was levelled, the turf replaced, and the lavender walks were planted to create a place of peace and tranquillity that, was at the same time a reminder of the 163 nuns whose bodies are buried there.

The outline of the graves and the colour of the grass show where they were laid. The grave markers were removed from the headstones and are now placed neatly along the length of the brick wall.

The two graves with kerbstones outside the Holy Thorn Chapel are the graves of 1) Abbess Caecilia Heywood, who died in 1931 and 2) Abbess Laurentia McLachlan who died in 1953

There is no particular order in which the graves are placed. These two graves are those of former Abbesses. The initial 'D' stands for 'Dame', which title was given to solemnly professed choir nuns. 'S' stands for Sister and is the title of a lay sister, junior or novice nun.

The Garden of Remembrance today: - JRH

THE CEMETERY

The cemetery area was originally part of the lawn in front of the old Stanbrook Hall. It was in use as a cemetery from 1878 when the first four nuns were buried there. In 1880 it was laid out and enclosed with the yew hedge. It was consecrated that year by Bishop Ilsley (auxiliary bishop in the archdiocese of Birmingham).

There is no particular order in which the graves have been placed. The two graves by the wall of the chapel are those of former Abbesses. The initial "D" stands for Dame, which is the title given to solemnly professed choir nuns. "S" stands for Sister and is the title of a lay sister, junior or novice nun.

As well as the nuns buried here there are also a number of "secular" graves. These include Harriet Berkeley, 1878, who lived in the village and was a great friend and benefactress of the community and Hannah Eccles, 1879, "our good and devoted servant".

The grave of Fr Laurence Shepherd, chaplain (1863-1885) and great benefactor of the community, is in the Holy Thorn Chapel. Other chaplains lie in the Mortuary Garden. Two pupils from the school are also buried in the mortuary: Elizabeth James who died in 1849 aged 15 and Angela O'Keefe who died in 1851, aged 9.

PLOT 2

D EDITH BARNECUT 31.5.1997
S LUCY BENNETT 1.3.1900
S BAPTISTA BIRCHALL 2.5.1899
D TERESA BRADLEY 26.8.1917
D THERESE BUREY 4.5.1988
D CECELIA BUTTI 24.5.1944
D JUSTINA CARY 29.5.1961
D ROSALIE CARY 30.4.1932
D MAURA CHAMBERS 13.11.1906
S MARTHA CHEW 14.10.1878
S ANNE FINNEMORE 21.12.1912
S GENEVIEVE FLICKER 6.3.1900
D CLEMETINA FREEMAN 22.12.1906
S BENEDICTA GLOVER 26.9.1901
S FRANCES GREEN 9.1.1916
M WALBURGA HAIGH 4.5.1930
S MONICA HEARN 1.4.1903
S EBBA HEIDEN 8.7.1936
S JOSEPHINE HORRIGAN 15.10.1936
M ANGELA HOULGRAVE 7.3.1915

CORNER PLOT BY CHURCH

D CAECILIA HEYWOOD 7.11.1931
D LAURENTIA MCLACHLAN 23.8.1953

D HILDEGARDE JANSEN 7.12.1926
D PAULA KEARNEY 19.6.1903
D FRANCIS KENYON 20.3.1954
D ALOYSIA KIERNON 5.9.1911
D MARCELLINA KIRWAN 4.1.1930
S BENEDICT LARKE 6.7.1920
S MARY ANN MCARDLE 5.9.1888
S EMERENTIANA MCGRATH 18.12.1924
D MONICA MORDLE 6.12.1878
D JULIANA MURPHY 24.3.1923
S MARIANNA PEET 25.6.1911
S CATHERINE PROSSER 15.5.1892
S BIBIANA REES 29.2.1908
D FRIDESWIDE SANDEMAN 12.11.1996
D MONICA SEE 26.11.1993
S ELIZABETH TALBOT 18.1.1900
D AGATHA THOMAS 24.12.1915
D BERNARD TIDMARSH 21.4.1906
D MONICA WATTS 20.1.1970
D URSULA WINKFIELD 2.2.1888

The plaque on the graveyard wall giving some details of the graves which are still here today: -JRH©

†
D. XAVERIA HODGES
DIED 17TH FEBRUARY 1908
AGED 83
R. I. P.

†
HENRIETTA BERKELEY
DIED 26TH NOVEMBER 1878
AGED 51
R. I. P.

Two plaques on the Churchyard wall, including Henrietta Berkeley who lived in the village and was a member of the prominent Catholic family of 'Berkeley'. She was a friend and benefactress of the Community here at Stanbrook. : -JRH©

For the last two years of her life, Harriet Berkeley lived at Stanbrook; she lived in the guesthouse known as the 'Hermitage' which was a few years from the front door of the Abbey, hence her burial in the monastery cemetery.

Some of the other plaques which once marked the graves of the community nuns at Stanbrook: -
JRH©

The cemetery of the former abbey now laid down to grass. It has lavender lined pathways to make
this area of the hotel a tranquil peaceful area for the hotel guests: -JRH©

The Earlier Burial Ground – known as the 'Mortuary' was in use from 1838 until 1878. '(Mortuary' has changed its meaning over the centuries (in the 20th and 21st centuries), where bodies are buried to a room were bodies are temporarily stored.)

The land that in 1878 became the cemetery, the newer burial ground, had been part of the lawn in front of Stanbrook Hall (as also of the 1838 monastery).

The earlier burial ground, the mortuary, was behind the former Stanbrook Hall and the 1838 monastery.

There is another cemetery area, which once formed part of the lawn in front of Stanbrook Hall. It was in use as a cemetery from 1878 when the first four nuns were buried here. In 1880 it was laid out and enclosed with a yew hedge. It was consecrated that year by Bishop Ilsley (auxiliary bishop in the archdiocese of Birmingham).

The ancient stone steps leading down from the side of Stanbrook Hall to the grassed area containing the first cemetery. Notice the different types of brick, relating to earlier buildings on this site.

The difference in the brickwork is interesting and the reason for this being that there were two cottages and a blacksmith's shop on the site before Richard Case built Stanbrook Hall in c.1755. There are traces to be seen of the two cottages on 1) the south side of the Presbytery/Bride's Manor incorporates one of them, b) the other cottage was south of the south wing of Stanbrook Hall.

In 1835, when the nuns bought the property, there were already detached offices, stabling for six horses, a double coachhouse, a cattle shed, and walled gardens. It is therefore no surprise to note the different brickwork here and elsewhere to the south of the residential buildings.

The two children buried in this mortuary burial ground were Elizabeth James in 1849 aged 15 years and Angela O'Keefe in 1851 aged 9 years.

The monument erected to mark the eight graves of the bodies brought from Abbot's Salford in 1838 when the nuns moved to Stanbrook. One of them is affectionately known as the 'Peppermint Man.' The bodies were actually buried between the stone monument and the gate of the walled garden. A Latin inscription was cut on the two sides of the monument in their memory: +Requiem aeternam Dona eis Domine+ that is 'Eternal rest grant unto them, O Lord.'-JRH©

The story according to Sister Philippa of Stanbrook (Wass) told also in 'A Great Tradition' – John Murray, 1953 by a Benedictine of Stanbrook – Dame Felicitas Corrigan tell the story of the tomb and the inundations in the grassed over older cemetery.

The name of the man in the tomb is Fr Augustine Lawson and he was revered as a saint while he was still alive. His coffin and those of seven of the nuns who had died while the community was at Abbots Salford in the Cotswolds, were exhumed and brought, illegally of course to Stanbrook Hall. In point of fact the bodies were moved before the actual community moved here themselves. They were buried in what used to be called the 'Old Mortuary' at Stanbrook. The workmen were supervised by a lay sister named Sister Mary Ann McArdle. The workman and the sister, to their surprise found that Fr Lawson's coffin was in perfect condition, as if he had only just been buried. They prised off the lid and found his body was in no way corrupted – 'lay there serene and peaceful as if only asleep, his habit and stole quite untouched by damp or mildew, while a scent of inexpressible sweetness exhaled from the body and the grave.' One of the workmen later described the fragrance to the archivist as – 'something like peppermint, sweet as the peppermint plant Ma'am.'

The mortuary, showing the concrete altar that served as the main altar in the abbey church from 1971 until 2009, and the mortuary chapel, known as the 'Little Hermitage' a place of prayer:-JRH

The Little Hermitage

An 1868 watercolour of the early graveyard on the south end of the site: - Grateful thanks to Sister Philippa Edwards and Sister Margaret Truran for permission to reproduce this photograph from the Stanbrook Abbey Archives©

The little chapel originally had glass doors as shown in the watercolour. It was furnished with panelling and seating (all in one piece) running the length of the south wall; also a pedestal, on which were placed a crucifix and an hourglass to indicate the length of time for prayer. In addition to the liturgical services that punctuate the day, the nuns prayed privately for half-an-hour in the morning and half-an-hour in the evening, hence the use of the hourglass. The little chapel or hermitage was used in the summer as an alternative place of prayer.

There are thirty two bodies buried in the mortuary, including those of two children, Elizabeth James and Angela O'Keefe, and of Abbess Scholastica Gregson who was responsible for the erection and consecration in 1871 of the Pugin Abbey Church.

Alongside the old graveyard is the old brick doorway into the garden area of the former mansion-Stanbrook Hall: - JRH

The garden wall from the former Stanbrook Hall - the fine handmade bricks contrast with the bright red bricks of the abbey walls: - JRH

The stone steps and the wooden seats alongside the lake where the nuns would have sat and meditated on a warm day in spring or summertime: - JRH

The Great Hall, the former church, with the altar still in position after the departure of the nuns for Wass. When Clarenco bought the property the altar was removed.: - courtesy of Neil Styles©

The lake where once the nuns could have sat down and enjoyed a time of quiet contemplation. In front of the lake, today's lawns would have been cultivated ground where vegetables were grown for the use of the community

The garden area where once vegetables and other crops were grown for the use of the abbey. The former chicken houses and farm equipment sheds remind us that the former abbey was pretty well self-sufficient: - JRH

The old poultry sheds at Stanbrook where chickens were reared. Poultry was an important food source providing eggs and meat for the community meals

The unusual wind vents on the chicken sheds

The nuns also had free-range eggs from hens which were kept in purpose-built sheds, so the hens could wander about and eat pests on the field containing cultivated vegetables and fruit. Today this is an enormous mound, where much of the rubble and soil was placed when the renovations took place when the abbey changed from its religious community use to a modern hotel.

One of the original 'free-range' chicken sheds positioned on the edge of the vegetable and crop fields of the abbey

Close by is Moat House Farm which belonged to the abbey, and helped to provide milk to supply the daily needs of the nuns. The farm was not a large source of income. The nuns depended on rents from the surrounding properties to help provide an income.

The nuns had their own farm buildings including a dairy and pigsties. They were pretty well self-sufficient in terms of supplying food for the community, which at one time numbered in the region of 80 nuns.

Moat House Farm close by the abbey:-JRH

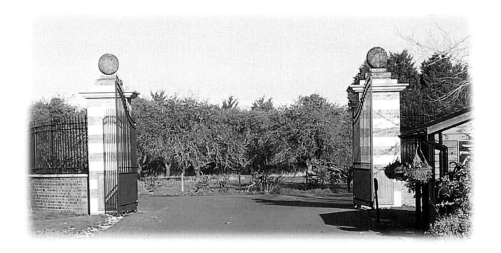

The present entrance gates to Stanbrook Abbey Hotel

The entrance gates today cut through the brick wall which enclosed the abbey and ensured that the community was separated from the world outside. On the inside of the wall is a walkway, which may have been the old 'Jennet Tree Lane' an ancient 'trackway'. The lane can be seen clearly and winds through the grounds amongst the variety of different trees the nuns planted, many having to be cut back or felled when the nuns finally left in 2009 as the grounds had become very overgrown and neglected. Here in the spring is a show of bluebells and snowdrops and also in their time multitudes of daffodils, much now covered with a modern car park. Here also to the side of the abbey itself was where the washing lines were sited and the beehives, as the bees were propagated above all for pollination, and the production of honey was a sideline.

The ancient trackway leading through the trees alongside the perimeter wall at Stanbrook, a mass of wild flowers in the spring and a haven for wildlife at all times of the year

Elm tree struck by lightning taken in 1907 & cutting the pasture close to Stanbrook Abbey c1912: -
courtesy of Ray Jones©

An early view showing the hay being harvested in the fields, just outside the abbey grounds: courtesy
of Ray Jones©

Some of the garden furniture at Stanbrook Abbey: - JRH

One of the fine red brick enclosure walls on the east side of the abbey: - JRH

St Mary's House

The retreat house – St Marys:-JRH

On the east side and alongside one of the entrances to the old front entrance of the abbey is St Mary's house which is a retreat house for those wishing to visit and stay at Stanbrook. The earliest part of the building was known as the *Hermitage*. It was built in 1865 and resembles a small Georgian style house. From 1911 the tenants of the Hermitage often took guests. In the early 1950s it was opened as regular guesthouse for the Abbey. Abbess Joanna Jamieson had the idea of building an extension with a large dining-room, to provide a retreat house. Officially opened in 1986 by Cardinal Basil Hume, it was renamed St Mary's.

The Eastern side of the Abbey with the 'Boulton' statue of St Peter, holding his keys: -JRH

The fine red brick east side of the abbey with each window being framed with Boulton carved heads featuring kings and queens, bishops, nuns and monks: - JRH

The visitors' Side entrance of the abbey: JRH

To the rear of the main abbey buildings and alongside the older Stanbrook Hall which now forms part of St Anne's Hall and the modern 'Bride's Manor' are several old farm buildings, the former stables of the Hall. These were used by the nuns for various workshops, for repairing and for pleasure.

These buildings are the stables and the coach houses of Stanbrook Hall. The bailiff was housed in the eastern part. The part later known as the Market Hall served as a laundry for the nuns until the building of the north wing of the Pugin monastery. Otherwise the buildings were used as workshops, by workmen employed as regular staff, and by the nuns for carpentry, woodcarving, art studios, etc.

The workmen employed to carry out regular maintenance and repairs had similar workshops for carpentry; so too did some of the nuns.

The entrance to the 1838 abbey lay to the south, where two matching octagonal buildings were erected in 1849 to serve as a lodge and a lodge stable at the entrance to the drive. They were connected by a gateway, linked with both buildings by flying buttresses. Only the buttresses and one of the piers survive.

The surviving pier with its large cross and stone urn on the top. The urn was originally surmounted by another cross: -JRH

The 19th century lodges at Stanbrook Abbey

There is a pair of 19th century lodges to Stanbrook Abbey, built of red brick with stone dressings with a slate roof. Each has a semi-octagonal plan with extensions at the rear. They are of two storeys with quoined windows. The doorways face the drive and between the lodges are two octagonal brick gatepiers with stone urns. Between these and the lodges are pedestrian gateways with arches treated as flying buttresses. The gatepiers are today connected by a brick wall.

The two lodges at Stanbrook Abbey c1920: - courtesy of Ray Jones©

St Wulstan's, as the Lodge proper came to be known, served when it was first built as a guesthouse. It also provided schoolrooms for the Catholic boys and girls in the village, and the schoolmistress boarded in the Lodge. From 1872 to 1879 the Stanbrook outsisters lived there. In 1879 the Lodge was tenanted, and the school lessons must have come to an end.

The Village School at Callow End with all the children looking excited at having their photograph taken! : - courtesy of Ray Jones©

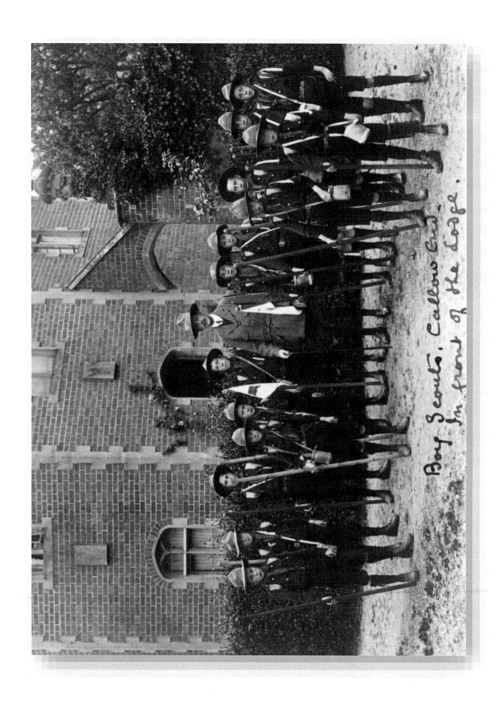

The local Boy Scouts at Callow End in front of the Lodge Gates to Stanbrook Abbey: - courtesy of Ray Jones©

Postcard views of Stanbrook Abbey in the 1920s and early 1930s: - courtesy of Ray Jones©

A more modern view of Stanbrook Abbey and of the entrances to the hotel in 2018

Stanbrook Abbey Hotel: - courtesy of 'Handpicked Hotels©

* *

Chapter Five: Stanbrook Abbey in Yorkshire

In May 2009, the community of nuns who were left at Stanbrook Abbey in Callow End, Worcestershire, made the decision to move to a purpose-built monastery at Crief Farm, Wass, in Yorkshire. It was a major and carefully thought out decision. Due to the community being so reduced but still numbering 25, it had become more difficult to service the enormous building at Stanbrook in Callow End and after being resident there for over 150 years Crief Farm was chosen, which is just north of Wass on the south-facing slopes below Wass Moor within the *North Yorkshire Moors National Park*. The site was chosen both for its isolation and reasonable accessibility. The proximity of *Ampleforth Abbey*, another Benedictine monastery, enables the monks to come in turn to celebrate daily Mass for the nuns. The new monastery is called 'Stanbrook Abbey'.

Ampleforth Abbey in North Yorkshire

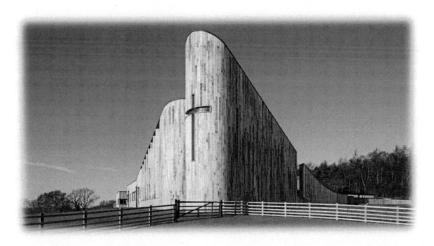

The modern and unique building of the new Stanbrook Abbey, Wass, North Yorkshire

The new monastery is ecologically and environmentally friendly. The nuns' new home in Yorkshire continues in the tradition of self-sufficiency and will allow the nuns to retain their shared vision of a life of prayer, living close to the land and being open to all genuine seekers of truth. The company chosen to design the new monastery was the company of Fielden Clegg Bradley Studios.

Part of the new Stanbrook – designed by the company of Fielden Clegg Bradley Studios

Fielden Clegg Bradley Studios (FCB Studios) – is a British

architectural design firm, established in 1978. The headquarters of the firm is in both Bath and London with offices in Belfast and Manchester. The company is particularly noted for its use of solar and sustainable design.

In 2008, 'Accordia' which was also designed by Alison Brooks Architects and Maccreanor Lavington, became the first housing development to win the 'Royal Institute of British Architects (RIBA) Stirling Prize.

'Accordia' is the Alison Brooks Architects designed Brass Building on Kingfisher Way in Cambridge

The company was founded originally in Bath in 1978 by the architects Richard Fielden (1950-2005) and Peter Clegg. The company originally designed and constructed low-energy houses. Over the next two decades the company won awards for the number of school design projects and gained 'a formidable reputation in the education sector' (The Independent 2016). Fielden was accidentally killed by a falling tree in 2005 and the company continued under Peter Clegg and the senior partner Keith Bradley.

Some of the notable projects that have been completed include:

- 2017 - Royal Birmingham Conservatoire, Birmingham.
- 2016 - Art and Design Building, Bedales School, Steep, Hampshire. Stanbrook Abbey, new abbey buildings in North Yorkshire, given a RIBA National Award in 2016.
- 2012 – The Hive, Worcester, housing the Worcestershire County Council public library and the University of Worcester's academic library.

The Hive in Worcester

- 2011 – Jodrell Bank Discovery Centre, Jodrell Bank Observatory, Cheshire.

Jodrell Bank telescope and the Broadcasting Tower, Leeds

- 2009 – Broadcasting Tower, Leeds, a student housing complex at Leeds Metropolitan University.
- 2008 -Accordia housing scheme, Cambridge.
- Derby QUAD.
- 2001 – Persistence Works, Yorkshire 'ArtSpace' building.

- 1999 – Aston University Lakeside complex.

Stanbrook Abbey – Wass, North Yorkshire

The new Stanbrook Abbey was described in the RIBA National Awards citation as '*A truly extraordinary piece of architecture...*' To execute such a beautiful organic form perhaps in the words and thoughts of the nuns who were going to live there meant that the splendid new architecture suggested divine intervention. The new building '*sits majestically within the woodland, rising out of the ground to form the crescendo to the plateau.*'

The Abbey is the new home for the *Conventus of Our Lady of Consolation*, a Benedictine community of nuns, who devote their lives to study, work and prayer, as did the nuns and monks of medieval times, who followed the same rules of St Benedict.

The new Stanbrook stands in the peaceful woodland of the North York Moors Park, a fairly isolated site chosen for its special and unique quality of 'silence and light.'

It was also remembered when this site was chosen that Benedictine Orders were established here before the Reformation and the tradition of monasteries can be seen close by which include *Rievaulx, Byland* and *Ampleforth.* One of the most stunning, is *Fountains Abbey* itself.

Fountains Abbey: courtesy of the Yorkshire Times©

Rievaulx Abbey in Yorkshire

The nuns at Wass live a simple, disciplined life and the new building, which was designed by the architect Fielden Clegg Bradley Studios, reflects this in every way. The main living areas are set around a cloistered courtyard, while the church and chapel, with their unique sinuous roof forms are clad with vertically placed oak boards, and give the appearance of rising out of the surrounding landscape.

The Central Courtyard with the cloisters surrounding this area. There is lots of light and glass to complement the design: - courtesy of the Wass Community at Stanbrook Abbey©

The paved courtyard with the surrounding glass cloisters, full of light

The internal spaces in the abbey are simple, tranquil and full of natural light and incorporate in their construction sustainable materials which include sycamore, Douglas fir and oak. The nuns have stated themselves that *'this is the place devoted to contemplation, where they could pray always.'*

The Church at Stanbrook filled with light and simple charm

The church with its sloping beamed roof which rises higher the closer you get to the altar. The large glass windows reflect the light at different times of the day and in different seasons and give a view to the surrounding countryside and its rare beauty: - courtesy of Peter Cook and Tim Crocker©

The nuns had a very specific brief for the new building; a monastery for the 21st century, which would be economical to run and sensitive to environmental concerns.

As part of the design it was stipulated that part of the monastery was to be entirely private and other areas were to be fully available and welcoming to the public. Access to the building is from the east side and the views and sunshine are to the south. All public, shared areas are therefore on the east side of the building, with service areas to the north, leaving the west and south sides to enjoy uninterrupted privacy and views.

The new abbey was built in two specific phases from 2007 to 2015. The private monastic areas, including the refectory and kitchen, Chapter House, Calefactory (common room) and other offices are arranged around a central courtyard/cloister. It leads to a row of 26 private cells for the nuns on two floors which run along the southern edge of the site, each with an en suite shower room, small outdoor space and beautiful views over the Yorkshire Wolds. Upper floors contain the house workrooms and a temporary library. The public areas including the 'parlours', where the nuns can meet their friends and the public, are beside the main entrance on the east side, next to the church and the chapel which are open to the public.

The Church – The nuns attend church services six times a day from before sunrise to sunset, just as the monks and the nuns would have done in the early monasteries in medieval times. The architect explains that '*Our intention was that this space – their home for so much of their lives – should change throughout the day and with the light of the seasons. Morning light would illuminate the curving wall to the north from a curved roof light and a vertical shaft of glazing towards the east. As the sun moves round it would be reflected off the timber columns which form the south-glazed wall until in the afternoon, when the light would enter from the south-west to bathe the whole church in light.'*

The north wall of the church rises from the congregational entrance and curves upwards to the high point of the altar, evoking what the nuns refer to *'as a sense of transcendence.'*

The south wall is composed of a series of slender spruce glulam columns with glazing between them. The columns are set at 60 degree angles along the wall to reflect and filter the light. The glazing frames are concealed so that the glass appears to span from column to column. To enhance the effectiveness as solar shading, each column has an integral non-structural glulam fin which extends externally, clad with vertical oak boards. At the ceiling the columns are fixed with concealed connections to a series of exposed glulam beams which support the roof.

Glued laminated timber, also called 'glulam' is a type of structural engineered wood product comprising a number of layers of dimensional lumber bonded together with durable, moisture-resistant structural adhesives.

View of the Church at Wass

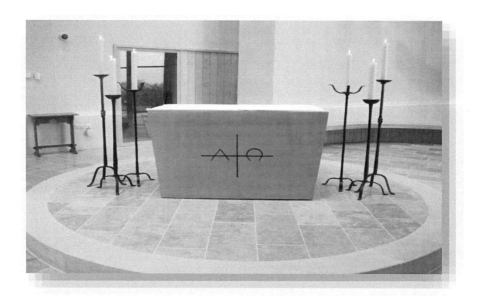

The Altar in the Church at Stanbrook: - courtesy of Sister Philippa Edwards and the Wass Community©

The Structure: - The organic, curved forms of both the church and the chapel were formed from 250mm thick reinforced concrete walls, cast in situ. The curved concrete wall of the chapel rises from 6 to 16 metres; it incorporates a glazed cross-shaped opening at its tallest point and then curves sharply back to form the north wall of the church, giving support to the glulam beam roof structure.

The reinforced concrete walls of the church and chapel

The curved 250mm reinforced concrete walls of the church and chapel are clad with an insulated rain screen of 125 x 25mm sawn untreated oak boards, PEFC certified and sourced from Germany.

Inside the church, the walls of the entrance space are clad with sycamore boards and the ceiling of the main church is lined with tongued and grooved Douglas fir boards. Sycamore, sourced from the UK, is used for the church choir stalls and the enclosure and framework of the organ. All the timber within the church and chapel is treated with AURO natural organic wood stains.

Seating and the bespoke sycamore organ

Sustainability: - The nuns of Stanbrook when designing and planning what they really wanted at the new Stanbrook, were very keen that the building would be both economic to run and ecologically sensitive in design. Preference was given to renewable, recycled or low embodied energy materials, and the nuns were particularly interested in minimizing their ecological footprint.

The new building therefore was to be highly insulated with plenty of natural light. Low energy appliances and fittings were installed; there was a rainwater collection for flushing the WCs and for the laundry room, a woodchip boiler, solar panels to preheat hot water and a reed bed sewage treatment system. A sedum roof was important for reducing water run-off.

Natural ventilation was to be used throughout the monastery, including the church and the chapel. The suspended floor of the church forms part of a passive stack ventilation system; fresh air is drawn in from below floor level, passes into the church via grilles beneath the windows and is extracted through roof vents at high level above the altar. Three opening windows towards the back of the church provide additional individual control.

* *